# MANAGEMENT OF AGRICULTURAL AND NON-AGRICULTURAL COOPERATIVES

# MANAGEMENT OF AGRICULTURAL AND NON-AGRICULTURAL COOPERATIVES

*By*

**Dr. S.Nakkiran**
*Professor*
*Department of Cooperatives*
*Institute of Cooperatives & Development Studies*
*Ambo University*
*Ambo, Ethiopia.*
*Email: doctorsnakkiran@gmail.com*

*&*

**Dr. M. Karthikeyan**
*Assistant Professor*
*Department of Cooperatives*
*Faculty of Business & Economics*
*Hawassa University*
*Hawassa*
*Email: mkeya2003@gmail.com*
*mkeya2003@yahoo.com*

DPH

**DISCOVERY PUBLISHING HOUSE PVT. LTD.**
**NEW DELHI-110 002**

*Published by:*

**Tilak Wasan**

**DISCOVERY PUBLISHING HOUSE PVT. LTD.**

4383/4A, Ansari Road, Darya Ganj
New Delhi-110 002 (India)
*Phone* : +91-11-23279245, 43596064-65
*Fax* : +91-11-23253475
*E-mail* : parul.wasan@gmail.com
discoverypublishinghouse@gmail.com
*web* : www.discoverypublishinggroup.com

***First Edition:* 2012**

**ISBN: 978-93-5056-056-3**

**Management of Agricultural and Non-Agricultural Cooperatives**



***Printed at:***

***Shree Balaji Art Press***

***Delhi***

# Preface

Cooperatives today have spread their wings in all walks of our life and they have penetrated into the lives of people of all countries. The cooperative movement today has crossed more than one and half century. The movement has not spared any of the sectors of social and economic development and today we can witness more than two hundred different types of cooperatives. There is vast difference between the developing countries and developed countries in their growth, development and coverage of activities by the cooperatives. Today in all developing countries we could find a growing cooperative movement working to solve problems in the basic fields of agriculture, small-scale industries, handicrafts, housing, consumer sector and the service sectors. Ethiopia, being an agricultural country, needs the blessings of cooperatives to go ahead with self-sufficiency in food grains production and production of commercial crops. The pace of growth of the cooperative movement in Ethiopia is slow compared to other developing countries. This book deals with cooperatives of various types that are working in Ethiopia. Some cooperatives like processing cooperatives and agro-engineering cooperatives are added for knowledge sake.

In writing this book we faced several problems. Our book being the first of its kind, we could not get enough literature, as books on Ethiopian cooperatives are non-existent. We have done our best to give good coverage of cooperatives. We expect constructive comments from our readers to make improvements in the next edition. We thank all our friends and admirers who helped us in preparing this book at each stage. We are thankful and grateful to Parul Wasan, Discovery Publishing House Pvt. Ltd., New Delhi for publishing the book neatly under his renowned label for the cooperative knowledge community.

**Dr. S. NAKKIRAN**

**Dr. M. KARTHIKEYAN**

# Contents

# Part – I

## Management of Agricultural and Allied Cooperatives

# 1 Agricultural Cooperation

## Introduction

The term "agricultural cooperation" includes all those activities, which are organized on cooperative lines for helping the farmer in the professional capacity as a producer. This form of cooperation is of immense importance to developing countries — where agriculture is the main occupation of the people. In these countries agriculture suffers from a number of inherent weaknesses; for example:

(*a*) The individual farmer can't fight against the forces of market and is unable to obtain the economies of large-scale production by his own efforts. Majority of farms are small and are often scattered. In Africa and Asia, the average size of a family-farming plot is approximately one to three hectares. Many of these farms are hardly economically viable units. Because of the small size, the individual farmer is not at all in a position to influence the market on his own;

(*b*) The yield from investment in agriculture is on an average much below than that in industry or trade, because of:

  (*i*) high inherent risk involved in production due to climatic factors and other contingencies;

  (*ii*) the high percentage of fixed costs and the long production cycle, making the agriculture less flexible for coping up with sudden changes in demand;

*(iii)* a highly imperfect market, perishable nature of many agricultural products and the lack of sufficient and suitable storage and processing facilities owing to which the farmer is compelled to sell his produce immediately;

*(iv)* difficulties in getting various financial needs.

In developing countries these difficulties are increased by the predominance of the agricultural sector in the economy, by the frequent lack of diversification, i.e., the dependence on a smaller number of crops and by the envisaged rapid changes in agriculture from subsistence farming to the cultivation of cash crops to supply the growing urban population and to earn foreign exchange through export in order to finance development.

After having an idea about agricultural cooperation, and the sufferings of agriculturalists, we can explain various types of Agricultural Cooperatives.

**Important Agri and Agri-related Cooperatives**

Agricultural cooperatives are rendering number of services to the farmers like provision of agricultural credit, marketing services, processing services, irrigation facilities, and allied occupations like dairying and poultry. The following are some of the important agricultural and agriculture-related cooperatives organized by cooperatives in developed countries and developing countries.

1. ***Agricultural credit cooperatives***

   These agricultural credit cooperatives are organized from village level to the national level with various structures or tiers. They provide short-term, medium-term and long-term credit to the farmers. They provide banking facilities and attract deposits from the farmers. In many developing countries agricultural credit cooperatives are acting as multi-purpose cooperatives. By this process, in addition to agricultural credit, they undertake marketing, processing activities and distribute consumer articles to them.

2. *Marketing cooperatives*

   Marketing cooperatives supply inputs to the farmers and purchasing agricultural produces and sell them for a higher price to the farmers. Marketing cooperatives have removed the middlemen and brought lot of benefits to the farmers.

3. *Processing cooperatives*

   Processing cooperatives are organized to convert raw agricultural produces into a consumable form. Sugar cooperatives convert sugarcane juice into sugar; cotton-processing cooperatives gin the cotton and separate cotton and cottonseed. Like this, many of the agricultural produces are converted into value-added products.

4. *Irrigation cooperatives*

   Irrigation cooperatives are organized by farmers who do not have assured irrigation facilities. They extract water from various sources like canal, river, and ground water and distribute water to the farmers. Small farmers are highly benefited by such cooperatives.

5. *Dairy cooperatives*

   Dairy cooperatives provide assured income to the farmers. Many dairy cooperatives have organized processing units and through them they manufacture dairy products like cheese, butter, milk powder, etc.

6. *Fisheries cooperatives*

   Though fishery is a separate occupation, fisheries cooperatives are brought under the fold of agriculture-related cooperatives. There are two types of fishing, inland fishing and sea fishing. Inland fishing is undertaken in rivers, ponds, and lakes. Sea fishing is undertaken through modern mechanized boats.

7. *Agro-engineering cooperatives*

   Many small farmers cannot afford to purchase costly agricultural machineries like tractor, sprayer, duster, and harvester. Such machines are purchased by agro-engineering cooperatives and they are hiring them to the farmers. Through such efforts, agricultural activities are quickly undertaken.

## Merits of Agricultural Cooperatives

1. Agricultural cooperatives provide services and supplies to the farmers. Services like marketing, processing, and godown facilities are important for the farmers. Supplies include input supplies, agricultural credit, consumer articles, etc.
2. Agricultural cooperatives relieved the farmers from the exploitation of moneylenders, middlemen and other intermediaries.
3. Agricultural cooperatives supply all inputs at a reasonable price and sometimes below the market price to the farmers and they save lot of money.
4. Marketing cooperatives sell the produces of the farmers for a higher price and the middlemen role is minimized.
5. Processing cooperatives convert the raw agricultural produces into a consumable form and provide value addition to the products. This process helps the farmers to fetch higher price for their produces.
6. Agricultural cooperatives benefit the consumers by means of distributing the agricultural products at a reasonable price in the market.

## Agricultural Cooperatives in Ethiopia

1. The popular agricultural cooperatives in Ethiopia are primary agricultural cooperatives, cooperative unions, and irrigation cooperatives.
2. Primary agricultural cooperatives and cooperative unions supply agricultural inputs and sell the produce of the farmers. They are not undertaking any other activities.
3. Primary agricultural cooperatives are not providing agricultural credit to the farmers. On the other hand, in several villages, the cooperative members have organized separate Savings And Credit Cooperatives (SACCOs). They provide short-term credit and mobilize deposits from the members.
4. Cooperative unions are the strongest cooperatives in the field of agricultural cooperatives in Ethiopia. They have

affiliated the primary cooperatives as members. But in many places cooperative unions do not exist.

5. One of the notable features of agricultural cooperatives in Ethiopia is that no regional or national level federations of cooperatives have been organized. Because of this drawback, Ethiopian cooperative movement has not become a member of the International Cooperative Alliance (ICA).
6. Agricultural cooperatives in Ethiopia have to be registered under the Cooperative Proclamation number 147/1998. The Federal Cooperative Agency and the Regional Cooperative Bureaus guide the cooperatives.

**National and Agricultural Economy of Ethiopia**

*State of the Economy* (Environmental Protection Authority, 2003, Addis Ababa)

Agriculture is the mainstay of Ethiopia's economy. In the year 1999/2000 agriculture's share of the GDP was 43.3 per cent. Industry's share was 11.5 per cent while distribution and services had a share of 22.2 and 29.0 per cent respectively. Between 1988/89 and 1999/2000 GDP grew at an average annual rate of 5 per cent. When this is broken down into economic sectors, a growth if 2.5 per cent in agriculture, 5.3 per cent in industry, 6.3 per cent in the distribution sector and 8.3 per cent in other services is indicated.

Export trade in Ethiopia is mainly based on agricultural products, which account for 90 per cent of the total. Out of the agricultural products exported, coffee makes up 70 per cent, and out of the total export, its share is 60 per cent. Following coffee, leather and hides account for 12 per cent and chat (mirra or *Catha edulis*) for 7 per cent of export trade earnings.

**The State of Poverty**

Ethiopia is one of the least developed countries in the world. Between 1995/96 and 1999/2000, Gross National

Domestic Product (GNP) per capita was between Birr 600 and 819. As indicated in the *Africa Environmental Outlook* published by the United Nations Environment Programme (UNEP) in 2002, Ethiopia holds the 171st position out of the world's 174 countries based on the UN human development index. According to the study carried out in 1999, an estimated 46 per cent of the population is under the national poverty line, which is Birr 1.075 per annum. This means that 46 per cent of Ethiopians meet their basic needs on an average income of Birr 3 per day.

Ethiopia has developed a poverty reduction strategy designed to bring about economic and social development. The poverty reduction strategy designed to bring about food security, expansion of educational and health services, controlling HIV/AIDS, expansion of roads, improving water resources utilization and gender equality. In addition, the strategy also addresses environment and population issues. Expansion of foreign trade, capacity building, including enhancement of good governance, is also part of the strategy.

**Land Use**

The size of Ethiopia is 111.5 million ha. Out of this, 74 million ha or 66 per cent of the total area is suitable for agriculture. However, the actual size of land cultivated is estimated to be only 16.5 million ha or 14.8 per cent of the total.

**Water Resources**

Ethiopia is known as the water tower of North-East Africa. Surface water resources in Ethiopia flow in 12 major river basins. It is estimated that an average of 122.19 billion $m^3$ of water is annually discharged from these basins. The country's total ground water resources are estimated to be around 2.6 billion $m^3$. The waters of 11 of Ethiopia's rivers flow into neighboring countries. The amount of discharge that remains in the country is not more than 9 per cent.

The wetlands in the various parts of the country cover a total of 18,587 km$^2$. This is estimated to be 1.5 per cent of the country's area.

80 to 90 per cent of the water resources of the country are found in the Abay, Tekeze, Baro and Omo-Gibe river basins. An estimated 30 to 40 per cent of the country's population is estimated to live in these basins. On the other hand, while the population living in eastern and central Ethiopia is estimated to be 60 to 70 per cent of the country's total, only 10 to 20 per cent of the total volume of the country's water resources is estimated to be located there.

It is estimated that there are 3.5 million hectares of potentially irrigable land in the river basins of Ethiopia. When compared with 44 other African countries, the potential places Ethiopia fourth. However, because land developed for irrigation to date has not been more than 5 per cent of the potential, Ethiopia comes down to eleventh position for actual utilization of water resources for irrigation.

## Rangelands and Livestock Resources

Livestock production systems in the country can be categorized into three types. These are: modern dairy farms run by the private sector and governmental organizations; production based mostly on free-range grazing in the middle and higher altitude areas where mixed farming is practiced; and production by pastoralists in the lowlands. In 2000/01 Ethiopia's livestock was estimated to consist of 35.4 million cattle, 11.4 million sheep, 6.9 million goats, 4.9 million equines, 0.5 million camels, and 38.0 million chicken.

## Crop Resources

Due to the suitable natural conditions prevailing in Ethiopia, numerous crop species can be grown in the different climatic zones. An estimated 7 million smallholder farmers account for 97 per cent of the crop production. Private entrepreneurs and state farms produce the remaining 3 per cent. Available information indicates that before the late 1950s Ethiopia used to be a net exporter of cereals and pulses. However, since the late 1960s, domestic agricultural production has not been able to cover even the minimum basic per capita human food requirement. As a result, the deficit is being complemented through foreign purchase and food aid. Recurring drought and environmental degradation, among other, can be mentioned as factors that have led to this situation.

**Demography**

In 2002, the population of Ethiopia was estimated at over 67 million. Out of this 56 million (84.7%) was rural and 10.3 million (15.3%) was urban. Out of the rural population 28.57 million (50.2%) were males and 28.34 million (49.8%) were females. For the urban population, the figures were 5.13 million (49.8%) males and 5.17 million (50.2%) females.

**Education**

Education has an important role to play in a country's social and material development. According to the results of a study made in the year 2000, only 29.2 per cent of the population above 10 years of age could read and write. The literacy rate for the rural population is 27.7 per cent while it is 69.9 per cent for the urban population.

**Human-made and Natural Disasters**

The increasing frequency of drought occurrences associated with global warming has exposed all local, but especially rural, communities to great amounts of misery. They do not have time to recover from past droughts and rebuild their assets before another dry period. The people living in the northern parts and the lowland areas of the country have suffered most from its impacts. Drought has also become a major factor causing natural resources degradation and the exacerbation of the poverty. The drought of 2002/2003 has exposed 15 million people to food shortages.

In addition to drought, the spread of desertification has become apparent in many parts of the country. Forest depletion, serious damage to soil resources, reduction in animal productivity and animal products, reduction in the amount of, and disruption in, the distribution pattern of rainfall are major causes for the expansion of drought and desertification.

**Employment**

In 1999/2000, Ethiopia has a labour force of 43.6 million, which was 68.6 per cent of the total population of 63.5 million. Of that labour force, 7.3 million (16.6%) were urban and 36.4 million (83.4%) were rural. According to the results of the 1994 census, 88 per cent of all the labour force was employed in the agricultural sector in various governmental and non-governmental organizations. Out of the employed labour force 14.1 million were male and 10.8 million were female.

Studies made by the Central Statistics Authority show that, in terms of employment by economic sector, 79.8 per cent of the labour force is employed in agriculture, 3.9 per cent in trade, 4.4 per cent in industrial production and 3.5 per cent in the hotels and restaurants sectors.

**Agriculture**

Agriculture is the mainstay of Ethiopia's economy. Consequently the agricultural sector's share of the GDP is about 50 per cent. It is estimated that agriculture's share of total foreign exchange earnings amounts to 90 per cent. Agriculture is also a sector on which the country's food security depends while it also serves as a source of raw materials for agro-industries. An estimated 70 per cent of the raw materials required by large, medium and small agro-industries are acquired from this sector. About 85 per cent of the labour force is employed by this sector.

Agriculture in Ethiopia is mainly characterized by a rain-fed mixed farming system carried out by smallholder farmers using traditional agricultural methods and practices. These smallholder farmers utilize 95 per cent of all cultivated land and produce 90 per cent of the total agricultural production without considering coffee, which is primarily produced by smallholder farmers.

**Characteristics of Agricultural Goods**

1. *Small-scale production:* Agricultural goods are produced in small, medium, and large sized farms. But compared to industrial production the size is very small. The quantum of production produced by farmers is usually low in developing countries compared to the developed countries.
2. *Scattered production:* Agricultural lands are spread out throughout a country and the farms are spread out to farther places. But in the case of industries, in a small size area a factory can be organized and large production can be arranged.
3. *Seasonal production:* Unlike factory production, agricultural production is seasonal and crops can be grown only according to certain seasons. So, agricultural production is decided by seasons.
4. *Dependence of nature:* Nature plays the crucial role in agricultural production. Agriculture has to depend on rainfall, temperature, soil conditions, etc. Whenever rainfall is low or high, agricultural production suffers. Erratic changes in climatic conditions also adversely affect agricultural production.
5. *More bulky and less value:* Agricultural commodities are very bulky and to the quantity and weight of the commodity the value is very less. Due to this factor, difficulties arise in transporting agricultural commodities from one part of the country to the other part of the country. Transport costs add to the cost of agricultural produces.
6. *Perishable in nature:* Majority of the agricultural commodities are perishable in nature. Even food grains

like wheat, *teff*, maize, etc. can be kept only for few months. On the other hand products like vegetables, milk, flower, etc. are perishable in nature and cannot be kept for a long time. Hence, they have to be sold within short period.

7. *Supply factor:* Agricultural commodities are produced seasonally and supply reaches the market during particular seasons. Hence, they have to be stored and kept safely for the rest of the period. Modern stores are needed to store agricultural commodities from pest attack, rat attack, etc.
8. *Demand factor:* Demand for agricultural commodities cannot be increased suddenly like industrial products. But processed agricultural commodities may get good demand and surplus agricultural commodities can be exported.
9. *Dependence on agriculture:* In less developed countries and developing countries, majority of the population depends on agriculture whereas, in advanced and industrialized countries less percentage of population depends on agriculture.

**Agricultural Peculiarities of Ethiopia**

1. Ethiopia is traditionally an agricultural country and today, nearly 80 per cent of the population depends on agriculture directly or indirectly. The pressure on agriculture must be reduced by means of diverting the agricultural population for self-employment and industrial sectors.
2. In spite of majority of the population depending on agriculture, the country is not self-reliant in its food production. Food security is a major problem for the country. Nearly 10 to 15 per cent of the shortage is met by import every year.
3. The major food crops produced in Ethiopia are *teff*, wheat, barley, maize, sorghum, *enset*, etc. The commercial crops produced are coffee, cotton, sugarcane, *chat*, etc.

4. The agricultural geography of the country is divided into two, namely, highland countries and lowland countries. In highland countries, agriculture is prosperous and gets high rainfall. Lowland countries are covered by arid and semi-arid areas.
5. Ethiopia has 12 major rivers and 11 rivers are going out of the country. Water conservation for agricultural purpose has been neglected and the country has very few dams to store water. 70 per cent of the water flowing to Blue Nile is contributed by Ethiopian rivers. Only 5 per cent of the agricultural lands get assured irrigation facilities.
6. Landholding has its peculiarity in Ethiopia. During the Imperial period vast lands were held by few individuals. During 1974 the Derg government went to the extreme of completely nationalizing the agricultural lands. Even now individual ownership is absent and lands are given to the cultivators by the Federal Government through Peasant Associations. Absence of land right is one of the reasons for the low agricultural production and commercial agriculture in Ethiopia.
7. Coffee is the major export crop through which the government is earning majority of its foreign exchange. Ethiopia is the fifth largest producer of coffee in the world but major part of the produce is consumed locally. There are fluctuations in the international price of coffee during every frequent period.
8. The country is not having sound institutional agricultural credit and marketing institutions. Agricultural credit, the basic input for agricultural development is neglected in Ethiopia and there are no formal institutional agencies like agricultural credit cooperatives to look after the needs of the farmers. Likewise, farmers suffer for want of strong agricultural marketing cooperatives. The present activities of primary agricultural cooperatives and cooperative unions meet a fraction of the needs of the farmers.

9. Commercial agriculture is yet to take place in Ethiopia in the form of intensive cultivation. For intensive cultivation the farmers need inputs like improved agricultural seeds, chemical fertilizers, pesticides, marketing and processing services. These activities are not moving at a faster pace to meet the food security system of the country.
10. Agro-based industries are very less in Ethiopia. The country has vast potential for commercial crops like cotton, groundnut, sugarcane, tobacco, oil seeds, etc. But production and concentration over these crops are very less. Number of cotton textile industries can be organized with the promotion of cotton growing. Number of paper mills can be organized using the eucalyptus tree as the raw material. The country has to go a long way in these directions.
11. The country has well-organized agricultural research stations under the guidance of EARO (Ethiopian Agricultural Research Organization) and universities. Their work is admirable in the field of improved seeds, extension works, and the propagation of improved methods of agriculture.

**Summary**

- Agriculture is the mainstay of Ethiopia's economy. In the year 1999/2000 agriculture's share of the GDP was 43.3 per cent. Industry's share was 11.5 per cent while distribution and services had a share of 22.2 and 29.0 per cent respectively.
- Export trade in Ethiopia is mainly based on agricultural products, which account for 90 per cent of the total. Out of the agricultural products exported, coffee makes up 70 per cent, and out of the total export, its share is 60 per cent
- Agriculture in Ethiopia is mainly characterized by a rain-fed mixed farming system carried out by smallholder farmers using traditional agricultural methods and practices.

- In spite of majority of the population depending on agriculture, the country is not self-reliant in its food production. Food security is a major problem for the country. Nearly 10 to 15 per cent of the shortage is met by import every year.
- The country is not having sound institutional agricultural credit and marketing institutions. Agricultural credit, the basic input for agricultural development is neglected in Ethiopia and there are no formal institutional agencies like agricultural credit cooperatives to look after the needs of the farmers.
- Agro-based industries are very less in Ethiopia. The country has vast potential for commercial crops like cotton, groundnut, sugarcane, tobacco, oil seeds, etc. But production and concentration over these crops are very less.

**Self-learning Activity**

Try to answer the following questions on your own:

1. Discuss the merits of agricultural cooperatives.
2. What are the peculiarities of agricultural commodities?
3. What is the scope for agro-industries in Ethiopia?

# 2 Agricultural Inputs

## Agricultural Inputs and Role of Cooperatives

Generally, agriculture can be classified as primitive agriculture and modern agriculture. Under primitive agriculture, farmers follow traditional methods of agriculture and they heavily depend on nature. Deep ploughing, rotation of crops, application of manure, crop protection measures, scientific marketing systems, etc. will not be followed under primitive agriculture.

Under modern agriculture, farmers use improved seeds, manure and chemical fertilizers, follow crop protection measures, go for deep ploughing, rotation of crops, intensive cultivation by way of taking more than one crop in a year on the same land. Assured irrigation facilities are developed under modern agricultural system. To face the natural calamities, the farmers are given crop and cattle insurance under modern agriculture. Here below, we can see the important inputs needed for agriculture.

## Important Agricultural Inputs

Farmers are in need of the following inputs for their agriculture:

1. Improved seeds
2. Fertilizers (manure and chemical)
3. Pesticides
4. Fuel

5. Agricultural credit
6. Service inputs — marketing, processing, equipments, insurance, hiring of machineries, etc.

***Improved Seeds***

Improved seeds are one of the preconditions of modern agriculture and total agricultural production. Improved seeds developed in agricultural research centers have greater production potential and farmers must use them to increase their per hectare production. But there are certain issues relating to the availability of improved seeds:

(a) *Cost of the improved seeds:* Compared to the traditional seeds collected in the farms by the farmers, the improved seeds are costlier. But the production will be higher than the traditional farm seeds.

(b) *Timely availability:* The farmers must get the improved seeds well before the sowing season. So the cooperatives or other institutional agencies must take steps to provide the improved seeds even before the sowing season.

(c) *Multiplication of such seeds for future:* In certain cases, improved seeds may have to be imported from foreign countries. To multiply such seeds for the broader use of many farmers, it may take lot of time. This is one of the difficulties of improved seeds.

(d) *Finance required for the purchase:* As the improved seeds are costlier, the cooperatives or commercial banks must come forward to provide loans for the purchase of improved seeds. Otherwise, the farmers may find it difficult to apply such seeds to the farms.

***Fertilizer***

Farmers can use both manures and chemical fertilizers. Manure is obtained from cattle and it has become scarce due to the decreasing cattle population and the increased demand for fertilizers. So, the alternative for the farmers is to go for chemical fertilizers, which are manufactured in the factories. The tasks included in fertilizer are as follows:

(a) *Forecasting the demand by season, location, and type of fertilizer:* It is very difficult to forecast the exact demand for fertilizers. The use of fertilizer depends on the type of crop and the season on which they are going to cultivate such crops. Farmers may also be in need of various types of fertilizers like DAP, Urea, mixtures, etc. It is slightly difficult to assess the quantity of each fertilizer needed by the farmers.

(b) *Transport and distribution channels:* Chemical fertilizers are manufactured either in a particular country or imported by certain countries like Ethiopia. From the production center or the harbor terminal fertilizers are to be transported quickly and safely. Again, from the producer or importer, the fertilizers have to be distributed through the wholesalers, retailers, or cooperatives. An effective and efficient distribution channel alone can do good to the farmers. Cooperatives are the most suitable agencies to distribute fertilizers to the farmers quickly and at a reasonable price.

(c) *Credit needed to procure fertilizers:* Fertilizer, as an input is costlier. The farmers are in need of finance, which can be provided by cooperatives or commercial banks. Without such credit arrangements, small farmers and poor farmers cannot get fertilizer.

(d) *Advisory and demonstration services at the farm levels:* Farmers are in need of advisory services through extension workers about the type of fertilizer to be applied and at what time to be applied. It is the duty of the agricultural extension department to undertake such activities.

(e) *Cost of fertilizers:* When fertilizer is imported by private merchants, naturally the cost will be high. If fertilizer is imported by cooperatives and distributed through cooperatives, farmers get lot of benefits. For example, in Ethiopia, cooperative unions distribute the fertilizers below Birr 50 per quintal than the market price.

(f) *Effects relating to fertility of the soil, environmental degradation, etc.:* Continuous use of chemical fertilizers would be harmful to the soil. So, the farmers must complement natural manure with chemical fertilizers to keep the fertility of the soil intact and to avoid harmful effects of chemical fertilizers.

***Pesticides/Herbicides***

Intensive agriculture led to the application of improved seeds and chemical fertilizers, which resulted in the multiplication of pest attack on crops. Farmers are in need of the application of chemical pesticides, fungicides, etc. Certain issues relating to the application of pesticides are as follows:

(a) *The higher cost of pesticides:* Like improved seeds and fertilizers, the cost of pesticides is high. So, the farmers must be provided with credit facilities.

(b) *Implements needed for its application:* To apply pesticides, instruments like sprayers and dusters are needed. These are costlier and an ordinary farmer cannot purchase it for use. So, facilities must be made by agencies like cooperatives to hire such instruments.

(c) *Harmful effects of chemical pesticides on the crop:* Before applying the chemical pesticides, the farmers must consult the agricultural extension workers. Steps must be taken to avoid the harmful effects of chemical pesticides. Natural herbicides like neem powder can be substituted with chemical pesticides.

(d) *Environmental degradation:* Care should be taken that soil conditions are not spoiled by chemical pesticides. Chemical should not also pollute water and the environment. Too much chemicals may also not good for vegetables and fruits, which are consumed by human beings.

(e) *Immunity for the pest:* Continuous application of chemical pesticides may make the pest immune to such things, which may demand more dose of chemicals. Here, farmers have to be careful.

***Fuel***

Now-a-days farmers are in need of fuel like petrol and diesel to operate pump sets, tractor, harvester, etc. Electricity can supplement fuel in certain activities. Improved methods of agriculture demand assured irrigation facilities to the farmers. In remote areas, and in areas where canal or river irrigation is possible, farmers have to get the ground water through motor pump sets, for which fuel or electricity is needed.

***Agricultural Credit***

Agricultural credit is the basic input, which is called as prime mover for agricultural development. Through adequate credit farmers can purchase the needed inputs like seeds, fertilizer, pesticides, etc. A farmer is in need of three types of credit:

(a) *Short-term credit:* Such credit is needed for a period of 3 months – 15 months for the purchase of inputs, to meet farm expenses like the payment of wages, payment of electricity fees, taxes, etc.

(b) *Medium-term credit:* Such credit is needed for a period of 15 months – 5 years. Such credit is needed for the purchase of agricultural implements, purchase of cattle and milch animals, for the erection of pump sets, etc.

(c) *Long-term credit:* Long-term credit is needed for a period of 5 years – 15 to 20 years. It is needed to make permanent improvements on land like leveling of land, constructing bunds, fending the farmland, construction of farm shades, to dig wells and construct ponds for irrigation. It is also needed to purchase heavy agricultural implements like tractor, harvester, thresher, etc. Long-term credit is also needed to purchase new lands for extending farmlands.

*Service Inputs*

Farmers are need of service inputs like marketing services, processing services, transport services, hiring of agricultural machineries, insurance, etc.

Marketing is an important service needed for farmers. There are two types of marketing undertaken by marketing agencies, namely input marketing and output marketing: *(a)* Input marketing denotes the supply of improved seeds, chemical fertilizers and pesticides to the farmers. *(b)* Output marketing implies the selling of agricultural produces to the market. Cooperatives are considered to be the better agencies in providing marketing services to the farmers. Transport, grading, weighing, and storing are some of the services related the to marketing services.

Closely related to the marketing service is the processing service to be undertaken for the farmers. Through processing activity a raw agricultural commodity is converted into next form. For example, conversion of wheat flour from raw wheat is a processing activity. Through processing activity value addition is given to the farmers, which fetches a higher price to their produce compared to the selling of raw agricultural produces.

Hiring of agricultural machineries is one more service inputs needed for the farmers. As agricultural machineries are costlier, all farmers cannot purchase costly machineries. So, institutions like cooperatives can purchase such costly machineries and hire them to the farmers. Important agricultural machineries are tractor, sprayer, duster, harvester, etc.

Insurance is another important service to be given to farmers. To protect the farmers' crop from natural calamities, crop insurance has been introduced. To protect the livestock, cattle insurance has been introduced. Such insurance services are undertaken by cooperatives, commercial banks, and insurance companies.

**Nature and Problems of Supply of Inputs by Cooperatives**

With the development of modern scientific agricultural methods the dependence of the cultivator has largely increased during recent decades, on outside supplies. With a view to maintaining a constant flow of supply of essential agricultural services the farmers require efficient machinery. The private trader cannot possibly serve the purpose. The farmers therefore have to look to a cooperative society for supplying the required agricultural services. Such a society can help in keeping the prices of essential agricultural supplies at a reasonable level and also in supplying goods and services of proper type, standard and quality which are required by the farmer for his agricultural operations.

Agricultural supplies can be organized through cooperatives. They collect orders from members and distribute them from door to door. One great advantage of such an organization is that the administrative cost is reduced to the minimum. The agricultural cooperatives society may have a number of functions. It may engage in the supply of basic farm requisites, e.g. artificial fertilizers, quality seed, chemicals, tools, fuel, lubricating oil etc. The society has to maintain a stock of assorted supplies. The quantity of the commodity to be ordered will be determined on the basis of the estimated total demand for a particular period.

The size of the order will, therefore, depend on:

1. the period for which the demand has been calculated;
2. the available storage space; and
3. the available capital.

Then the society will have to make a useful study of the various sources of the supply of required articles. The offers received from various firms will have to be compared in respect of the price, terms of delivery, the terms of payment, the delivery schedule, the reputation and reliability of the firm concerned. It may be possible that the society may itself undertake the production of the necessary supplies, but in all cases it cannot be possible. The society may have to face a number of problems in respect of storage space. It is necessary that the society should have a good extension service. The society will have to take care of the fact that it will sell to its members the articles that they require. The type of extension service can be carried out.

1. by the society itself; or
2. by specialists employed for the purpose or obtain direct from the secondary organizations; and
3. by outside organizations like the farmers' unions, the Government departments, etc. Various methods used for such extension activities are: individual advice, organization of training courses. On-the spot demonstrations, lectures, film shows etc.

Supplies can either be delivered at the farms or collected by the members. Which one of the two to choose will depend largely on whether the society has the necessary transport facilities and is in a position to bear the cost of transport without increasing the price of the commodity, or the farmer is willing to pay the extra delivery cost. Besides,

1. the accessibility of the individual farm, the average distance between the member's farm and the society's premises and the means of transport available;
2. the average bulk and weight of each consignment; and (c) the presence of competitors will also have to be taken into account.

**Price Policy for Inputs and Supplies**

The price policy adopted by a society is of great significance and depends by and large on the mode of operation. A society acting as an agent for its members, does not necessarily frame its own price policy. A society, which buys articles for supplying to the members at its own risk and responsibility, is completely free to frame its own price policy.

The price policy will depend on:

1. whether the society should charge uniform prices from all member; and
2. whether the society should charge different prices from different members according to the size of the order, time or distance etc.

There can also be another basis for the calculation of the price and that is whether all the articles should be sold on the same percentage of commission or the percentage of commission should be different for different groups of commodities. The differential prices may be determined:

1. by distributing the total cost amongst single commodity group. This will be an objective approach and
2. according to the commodity groups, which allow high margins, are charged with the main bulk of expenditure without taking into account the true cost structure and the same will be to cover the total cost of operation. This will be a subjective approach.

**Agricultural Insurance**

Farming involves more risks than any other business since it is greatly dependent on climatic conditions. Moreover, crops can be seriously damaged by pests and diseases. Although by the application of modern farming techniques these risks can be kept at a reasonable level the farmer is never able to do away with them completely. Consequently, in developing countries the farmer's very existence is in danger. Agriculture has two types of insurance, namely crop insurance and cattle insurance.

Agricultural insurance schemes have been formed through cooperative effort in various countries for the protection of the farmers from these risks. Cooperative agricultural insurance society protects the farmer against losses and damage and acts as an additional source for the supply of capital for the cooperative movement. The success of such a society depends largely on the fact as to how far it is able to spread the risk over the widest possible area and the maximum number of members. Such societies have been organized at regional and national levels and sometimes they have a strong secondary system. In certain cases cooperative marketing societies are also engaged in providing insurance services to their members. These societies cover:

1. general risks, which the farmer faces, e.g., fire, life, accident, burglary etc.; and
2. specific risks inherent in agricultural operations. Cooperative insurance societies have also been covering the risk of other primary and secondary cooperative organizations. The risk can be covered by such societies either fully or partly. Full risk is covered when the crop or the animal involved is covered against all possible natural risks, while the risk is partially covered in the case of single or specific risks.

A particular risk to be covered is chosen on the basis of:

1. the relative economic importance of the crop or livestock covered;
2. the nature of the risk involved; and
3. whether the risk is assessable.

Agricultural insurance cooperatives also perform some other functions like:

1. Insurance counseling;
2. Assessment of insurable interest;
3. Under-writing of the insurance bills;
4. Inspection of the insured property;
5 The collection of premium; and
6. The processing of the claims.

The compensation offered for any loss or damage is generally less than the actual cost involved. The basis for such compensation in the case of crop insurance is either the long-term average yield per acre or the specific yields of a representative farm. The rate of compensation is usually progressive. Similar pattern is followed in livestock insurance. The premiums are calculated in such a way that the administrative cost and normal losses during the contract period are easily covered. In agricultural insurance abnormal risk has its own significance, because crop failures and epidemics are generally widespread. As the premiums are calculated on the basis of normal risks, the society has to make some provisions for covering abnormal risks. These provisions may be:

1. a strong reserve fund; and
2. reinsurance of a part or of the entire abnormal risks with other insurance organizations. In practice, a combination of both these provisions is found.

In developing countries, the problem of agricultural insurance is a ticklish one. There may be more than one reason for this:

1. It is not easy to calculate the risk accurately owing to the lack of statistical data;
2. Trained and qualified persons are not available for insurance work;
3. The risk involved is generally higher than in other countries owing to the ignorance of the farmer, outmoded farming techniques, inadequate veterinary services, low quality of livestock and dependence on climatic conditions;
4. Farmers can hardly afford to pay for insurance. It is because of these difficulties that agricultural insurance schemes have not gained much headway in these countries.

## Role of Cooperatives in Providing Agricultural Inputs in Ethiopia

There are various types of cooperatives that can provide various inputs needed by the farmers. The experience in developing countries have shown that one cooperative at the village level (multi-purpose cooperative) can provide all types of agricultural inputs and supplies to the farmers. But in developed countries separate cooperatives do individual services to the farmers. In Ethiopia, the primary cooperatives in collaboration with the cooperative unions distribute fertilizers and other inputs. To provide credit to the farmers, a beginning has been made by the SACCOs (Savings and Credit Cooperatives). The following are the observations of the cooperatives in Ethiopia in providing agricultural inputs to the farmers.

1. In Ethiopia primary cooperatives organized at kebele level are called by different names like primary cooperatives, producers' cooperatives, multi-purpose cooperatives, and service cooperatives. These primary cooperatives are primarily engaged in the distribution of fertilizers and the collection of dues for the cost of inputs. Unlike the other developing countries, primary cooperatives in Ethiopia are not providing agricultural credit to the farmers.
2. There are two types of primary cooperatives distributing inputs to the farmers. Under the first type, the primaries themselves procure the inputs in the market and supply them to the farmers. The second types of primary cooperatives are affiliated to the cooperative unions. The cooperative unions procure the inputs in the wholesale markets on behalf of the affiliated primary cooperatives and supply them to the farmers through the primary cooperatives.
3. The cooperative unions are bigger cooperative organizations meant for purchasing inputs to the farmers through the primaries and sell the agricultural produce

on behalf of the farmers. During the year 2006, eight cooperative unions in Oromiya region have got license from the ministry to import fertilizers directly from foreign countries. Through this process, they are able to sell the fertilizer for Birr 50 per quintal lower than the market price. The cooperative unions procure the farm produces from the farmers and sell them for a good price on behalf of the primary cooperatives and farmers.

4. Some of the NGOs in Ethiopia are promoting and guiding the agricultural cooperatives as per the Cooperative Proclamation 147/1998. Such NGOs have organized special types of cooperatives called "Seed Multiplication Cooperatives". These cooperatives are organized by the unemployed youth. They get improved seeds from the agricultural research stations through government quota. Afterwards, the seed multiplication cooperatives through their members multiply the seeds in the farms and sell them to the farmers. This process solves two purposes. The first one, the unemployed youth are able to get employment opportunity through seed multiplication and earn good income. Secondly, the farmers are able to get improved seeds at a reasonable price without any shortage in these areas.
5. One of the preconditions for the efficient distribution of inputs is the transport system. Many primary cooperatives and cooperative unions are not having their own transport vehicles. So, they hire the transport vehicles from the private operators. The transport cost paid for such purposes is very high and the cooperatives can think of purchasing their own vehicles by getting financial help from the commercial banks.
6. Another precondition for the successful distribution of inputs is the storage system. A cooperative should have adequate stores or godowns to keep the stock safely and to distribute them throughout the season. Many cooperatives do not own their own stores and they hire

private godowns or government godowns, which are costlier. So, such cooperatives must plan to construct their own stores in future and they can save lot of money.

**American Experiments in Input Supply through Cooperatives**

***Agricultural Cooperative Development in the United States***

The cooperative movement in the U.S. has been strongest in rural areas. Farmers have formed cooperatives for many purposes, including marketing of produce, purchasing of production and home supplies, and provision of credit. Farm marketing associations are the most important type of agricultural cooperative. Farm purchasing cooperatives rank second in importance. The modern farmer-member, who depends increasingly on off-farm products, can realize maximum savings by ordering goods through cooperatives. Regional cooperatives order some items from manufacturers and produce others in their own plants. The most important manufactures of these cooperatives are feed, fertilizer, and petroleum products; other cooperatively produced items include paint, lumber, and farm equipment. The cooperative petroleum industry is one of the most complex of the industrial enterprises; it includes oil wells, refineries, pipelines, storage facilities, and service stations.

Cooperatives account for a larger share of total economic activity in Europe than they do in the United States. However, they are nonetheless a fundamental part of American tradition - both past and present - especially in agriculture.

In 1752, nearly a quarter-century before the birth of the country, Benjamin Franklin, one of the signers of the Declaration of the Independence, helped start what is considered the first formal cooperative business in the United States.

**Growth Factors**

Many factors have been cited as major influences in the development of agricultural cooperatives in USA, but these factors logically can be grouped into three types, all inter-related:

1. economic conditions, whether produced by war, depression, technology, national economic policy, or the marketplace;
2. farmer organizations, including their leadership, their motivational capability, their enthusiasm for promoting cooperatives, their effectiveness in influencing public policy, and their longevity; and
3. public policy, as determined by presidential interest, by legislative initiative (at both state and federal level), and by judicial interpretation.

After the Civil War cooperatives were recognized as a feasible, self-help business alternative by agricultural producers. An early developmental factor was their promotion by the Order of the Patrons of Husbandry (commonly known as the Grange), the first of several general farm organizations. Founded in 1867 by a U.S. Department of Agriculture employee named Oliver Hudson Kelley, the Grange was conceived as a fraternal order to restore good feeling between people of the north and south.

Due to economic conditions of the time, however, the Grange's social function was quickly subordinated to an emphasis on cooperatives for economic improvement. Difficulties with early attempts at forming cooperative led the Grange to adopt the Rochdale system in 1875 and to distribute its rules to Grange stores. A burst of new cooperatives and reorganization of earlier joint-stock stores was short-lived as the Grange began to decline.

The Grange continues to exist today, occupying a philosophical position between the National Farmers Union and the American Farm Bureau Federation. The organization, has:

1. popularized cooperatives as a business concept throughout the nation;
2. proved the power of cooperative action;

3. demonstrated the value of the Rochdale principles, showing they could be applied to marketing as well as purchasing; and
4. identified the necessity of sound business management and operations.

As the Grange declined in influence, other farm organizations took their turn at fostering the development of cooperatives. Major ones, though short-lived, were the Farmer Alliance, formed in 1875, and the American Society of Equity, formed in 1902.

Another major farm organization, formed in 1902 and existing today, was the Farmers Educational and Cooperative Union of America, which evolved into the National Farmers Union.

Today's largest farm organization, the American Farm Bureau Federation, began in 1919. The American Farm Bureau and the National Farmers Union, by their long-term survival and organizational strength, have contributed the most among the farm organizations to the development of farmer cooperatives. Their support has been both in developing economic organizations and in exerting influence in the political arena.

**Federal Government Support to Cooperatives**

Before 1890 the U.S. policy towards cooperatives was neutral. Until that time, there were not many cooperatives and many functions without the attention of government. Since 1914 laws were passed to create favorable environment for cooperatives. In 1913 Theodore Roosevelt sent a commission to Europe to study the cooperative development. As a result, Federal Farm Loan Act was passed leading to the establishment of cooperative farm credit system. In 1913, U.S. Department of Agriculture established an office of markets and advisory programmes to cooperatives. Government encouraged the cooperatives actively during the period 1920 to 1932. Most of the states established cooperative legal systems during this period.

The Cooperative Marketing Act of 1926 broadened the U.S. Department of Agriculture's support and encouragement to farmer cooperatives.

It directed USDA (U.S. Department of Agriculture) to create a division of cooperative marketing for the purposes of:

*(a)* Collecting and analyzing historical and statistical data.

*(b)* Conducting studies of cooperation regarding economic, legal, financial and social aspects.

*(c)* Surveying and analyzing business practices.

*(d)* Helping farmers organize cooperatives.

*(e)* Collecting and analyzing data on agricultural production and marketing.

*(f)* Promoting the knowledge of cooperative principles and practices.

*(g)* Conducting other studies in the United Sates and in foreign countries that could prove useful to cooperative development.

The Agricultural Marketing Act of 1929 also included several provisions important to cooperatives. It provided for advisory commodity committees from cooperative associations. It established the Federal Farm Board with a major policy of expanding and strengthening the cooperative movement. It provided $500 million revolving fund to make loans available to cooperatives for marketing activities.

**Cooperative Growth in Response**

During the decades of 1920s and 1930s when government encouragement was high, many cooperatives were organized. In addition to farming, regional and inter-regional organizations, farmers organized national associations to provide commodity information, educational and other services and to influence legislation. Some of the examples of these associations are Cooperative League of USA (now the National Cooperative Business Association) and the National

Mild Producers' Federation (1968), American Institute of Cooperation (1925), National Council for Farmer Cooperatives (1925), Credit Union National Association (CUNA) (1934), and National Rural Electric Cooperative Association (1942).

During the period of cooperative growth, two major schools of thought on the role of cooperatives had developed. They were Sapiro monopoly approach and Nourse yardstick approach.

## SAPIRO MONOPOLY APPROACH

Sapiro was a California lawyer and he emphasized legalistic approach to cooperative business. The major points advocated by this approach were as follows:

1. Cooperatives should be organized around a single commodity, such as wheat or tobacco.
2. Membership should be restricted to agricultural producers.
3. A cooperative should maintain long-term contracts with its members.
4. A high proportion of the farmers producing a particular commodity should sign the contracts before the contracts take effect.
5. Products should be pooled, graded, and the member should receive a price based on the grade.
6. Cooperatives should adopt sound business principles and techniques.
7. Marketing should be spread over the year and not concentrated at harvest time.
8. Cooperatives should be organized on a centralized rather than federated basis.

## NOURSE YARDSTICK APPROACH

Nourse was a professor at Iowa State University. He felt cooperatives should operate in the capitalistic system. The following were the major guidelines for establishing such cooperatives.

1. Establish cooperatives with a bottom-up democratic base.
2. Develop cooperatives as an integral segment of the existing capitalistic system.
3. Build business efficiency of the total economic system.
4. Control a modest share of commodity, supply or service.
5. Keep other business forms competitive with cooperatives, service as a balance or yardstick and thereby correct many of the excesses associated with capitalism.
6. Preserve individual producer freedom of decision-making.
7. Limit government assistance to cooperatives primarily to legislation or in other words to establish the legal framework for the cooperatives.

**Characteristics of American Cooperatives**

The characteristics of the American cooperatives for the past years can be summarized as follows:

1. Government's approach to cooperatives has been to maintain an interest in cooperatives with minimal support in the form of advice, education, and research.
2. Friendly and complimentary relationship has been developed between general farm organizations and cooperatives.
3. Cooperatives have maintained neutrality with regard to political parties but they are assuming an increasing political action to influence farm policy, macro-economic policy and the business climate.
4. Economic conditions have been the dominant force influencing cooperative structure and business strategies.
5. Larger cooperative size has enabled the cooperatives to enter into further processing of agricultural products.
6. Although cooperatives have been involved in an international trade for more than a century, cooperatives are now trying to find alternatives for developing an international business strategy.

Virtually every phase of agriculture is touched by cooperatives either directly or indirectly. Over 2500 supply cooperatives — mine, drill, refine, process, manufactures, package and distribute feed, seed, fertilizer, petroleum, pesticides, and every conceivable farm supply to serve today's

*Estimated share of market obtained by farm cooperatives of USA*

| | 1950/51 | 1960/61 | 1969/70 | 1975/76 |
|---|---|---|---|---|
| ***Product marketed*** | | | | |
| Cotton and cotton products | 12 | 22 | 26 | 26 |
| Dairy products | 53 | 61 | 73 | 69 |
| Fruits and vegetables | 20 | 21 | 27 | 27 |
| Grain and soybeans | 29 | 38 | 32 | 40 |
| Livestock and products | 16 | 14 | 11 | 9 |
| Poultry products | 7 | 10 | 9 | 8 |
| Others | 15 | 22 | 27 | 27 |
| **Total** | **20** | **23** | **26** | **29** |
| ***Farm supplies purchased*** | | | | |
| Feed | 19 | 18 | 18 | 19 |
| Seed | 17 | 19 | 20 | 15 |
| Fertilizer | 15 | 24 | 32 | 36 |
| Petroleum | 19 | 24 | 26 | 28 |
| Other supplies | 5 | 7 | 9 | 9 |
| **Total** | **12** | **15** | **16** | **18** |

farmers. Nearly 20 per cent of all farm supplies are now sold through cooperatives, and this sales amount to over $9 billion annually. Marketing cooperative helped their members to sell nearly $30 billion worth of farm production in 1976 or nearly 30 per cent of the total national farm production. Finance cooperatives, through the farm credit system (production Credit Association, Federal Land Bank, and Bank for Co-ops), supply nearly $50 billion annually to help their members buy and operate their own farms and finance their businesses.

And a wide variety of service cooperatives aid farmers by irrigating their land, insuring their assets, improving their livestock, and providing electric power and telephone service for rural areas. American farmers hold a total membership of nearly 6 million in 77,535 separate cooperatives. Since there are only slightly under 3 million farmers in this country, many of them may hold membership in more than one cooperative simultaneously. Obviously, cooperatives are an important part of the American agribusiness community. Brand name such as Sunkist (citrus), Land or Lakes (dairy and poultry), Welch (grape juice), and Diamond (walnuts) are all cooperatives that market their members production through these brands.

In 1974 there was severe worldwide shortage of fertilizer. At that time, the federal government had imposed price controls to control inflation. United States fertilizer manufactures has the opportunity to sell their product on the world market at a price that was about three times greater than the controlled domestic price. Many noncooperative companies quickly move to reap high profit by selling significant quantities of fertilizer to foreign markets. Cooperative, however, were dedicated not to making huge profits but to providing their members with all-too scarce fertilizer. So cooperative sold all their fertilizer production to their members at the controlled domestic prices. In fact, some cooperatives even went so far as to purchase high-priced fertilizer from the world market for distribution to members of at the lower domestic price, in order to assure their members of an adequate supply. Thus, the orientation of cooperatives to ward meeting members' needs triggered a very different set of operating decisions from those of the non-cooperatives.

### The Organizational Structure of Agricultural Cooperatives in USA

The cooperative system in the United States is highly complex and inter-woven. It ranges from simple, local, independent cooperative to the inter-regional cooperative that link literally thousands of local and regional cooperative into one complex organization.

The local cooperative is usually organized as a corporation: thus it has the same general structure as any corporate organization. Stockholders elected a board of directors who, in turn, select a manager to carry out their policies than hires appropriate personal to perform prescribed duties.

Regional cooperative are conglomerations of local cooperatives. Joined together in rather a formal or informal manner. Their primary purpose is to provide manufacturing, and wholesaling services to local cooperatives. They are necessary because local cooperatives are often not large enough to compete effectively all the advantages of the United States large organization, which in turn lends the local more muscle in the market place. There are even a few national and international cooperatives.

There are two basic types of regional cooperatives: generated cooperatives and centralized cooperatives. Each has a different type of organizational structure, which greatly affects the way it operates.

Federated cooperative are really cooperatives whose members are other cooperatives, usually local cooperative, in conjunction with other locals, owns and controls the regional. The control is from the bottom up, with the regional responding to the voiced needs of the local cooperatives.

Centralized cooperatives differ in that the local cooperative outlet is controlled by the regional cooperative rather than by a local board of directors. In this case, local farmers elect regional directors, who control the regional cooperative which in turn manages and control the local cooperative outlet. There involved board of director's *per se* instead, there is usually a local advisory committee that communicates regularly with local management, which report directly to the regional cooperative management. Control is essentially from the top down.

Some regional are actually mixtures of federated and centralized organizations. That is, a regional cooperative may simultaneously serve some local cooperative outlet that are federated and others that are centralized. This often comes about because some locally owned and controlled cooperatives have gotten in to financial difficulty and have been taken over by the supporting regional to protect the financial interests of individual farmer members.

Today, about one-fourth of all farm inputs are supplied by cooperatives. Also, nearly one-third of all agricultural production is marketed through cooperative. Many Cooperatives. Even process and distribute their members' products directly to supermarkets.

**Affiliation Systems**

Efficiency and economy in the operation of cooperative enterprises are generally achieved by a system of affiliation and centralization. Local cooperatives are served and supplied by state or regional organizations. In many fields the regional bodies are united in national organizations, which, in turn, are federated into still larger national organizations, such as the American Institute of Cooperation, the National Council of Farmer Cooperatives, and the National Cooperative Business Association (NCBA). The NCBA provides a government lobby for the cooperative movement. Systems of affiliation are characteristic of the movement in all countries, and international affiliation coalesces around the International Cooperative Alliance, with headquarters in Geneva, Switzerland. In addition to cooperative effort within their own operations, cooperatives in the U.S. are assisting more cooperative development among low-income peoples at home and abroad. They have helped to form commercial fishing cooperatives, provide sewing machines, establish credit unions, set up programmes for loans and life and savings insurance, found cooperative housing, and couple economic-development projects with member-education programmes.

Some of these programmes have been aided substantially by contracts from the U.S. government and by grants from foundations.

**Summary**

- Farmers are in need of several inputs like improved seeds, fertilizer, pesticides, fuel, credit, and service inputs like marketing, processing, equipments, insurance, and hiring of machineries.
- Cooperatives are the suitable agencies to provide these inputs to the farmers.
- Cooperatives have to follow a different price policy by way of supplying inputs for a reduced price to the farmers.
- In Ethiopia, agricultural inputs are supplied by primary cooperatives and cooperative unions.
- Several cooperative unions join together and import fertilizers and sell them for a lower price to the farmers.
- Though America is capitalistic country, cooperatives are powerful in distributing inputs and doing service to the farmers.
- One of the freedom fighters, Benjamin Franklin took the initiative to form cooperatives in America.
- The federal government of USA had passed many legislations to promote cooperatives in USA.
- When there was a shortage of fertilizer in 1974, private traders sold for a very high price but cooperatives sold the fertilizer below the market price in USA.

**Self-learning Activity**

Try to answer the following questions on your own:

1. Discuss in brief inputs needed for agriculture.
2. Illustrate the price policy for inputs distribution?
3. What are the economic factors that influence the presence of agricultural cooperatives?
4. Explain the organization structure of co-ops in USA?

# 3 Processing Cooperatives

## Significance of Processing Cooperatives

Processing of agricultural produce is one of the important functions of agriculture, which provides value addition to the agricultural products. Processing implies the transformation of products from their non-usable form to usable form. Processing increases the value of the products and makes it possible to retain them for a longer period. It ensures their ready supply throughout the year and thus helps the stabilization of the price. In developing countries, processing is of immense advantage since it helps agriculture a profitable profession. But the individual farmer cannot undertake it owing to limited resources, in terms of finance, technical skill, and limited marketable surplus. Consequently, processing is undertaken by middleman in the private sector, who takes away the profit from the farmers. So, it is ideal to organize processing cooperatives by the farmers.

Processing can be done either by indigenous methods or by mechanical power. The former method can be of advantage only in those areas where unemployment or under-employment is rampant. But, in areas where there is shortage of manpower and where the problem is one of reducing the cost, processing by mechanical power would be economical. In Ethiopia, our chief problem is to create employment opportunities for the rural people. It is, therefore, necessary that labour-intensive methods are adopted for processing of agricultural produce. Hence, indigenous methods may be adopted in rural areas while mechanical power may be employed in urban areas. Again commodities, which are meant chiefly for export, may be processed with the help of mechanical appliances.

Processing cooperatives have been flourishing in the field of sugar, rice and fruit processing etc. These cooperatives involves huge amount of capital and managerial expertise. Processing cooperatives like the sugar cooperatives have become the growth centers and stimulate the growth of rural economy.

The importance of processing cooperatives has been pointed out by the Indian Committee on Cooperative Processing (1960/61) as follows.

> "Cooperative processing is an indispensable part of cooperative marketing, specially in regard to cash crops. So far, except in the case of sugarcane and sugar, cooperative processing has practically made no headway in the country. Successful marketing of such products on cooperative lines, is not possible unless their processing is also done cooperatively. In the opinion of the committee, the linking of credit with processing was not only equally vital to the linking of credit or marketing, but if adequately developed, cooperative processing could also augment large-scale expansion of cooperative credit particularly for cash crops."

Processing of agricultural commodities can take the following two forms:

1. A change in the appearance or substance of the produce achieved by extracting, pressing, separating, maturing and similar transformations carried out by dairy industries, coffee industries, cotton ginneries, grain and oil mills, and fruit juice factories.

2. An increase in the durability by canning, chilling, freezing, dehydrating, smoking, salting, or some other form of preservation.

**Circumstances that Favour the Organization of Processing Cooperatives**

1. ***Perishable nature:*** Agricultural commodities are perishable in nature. They should be sold or processed immediately. By processing, the life of such goods is extended. Perishable products like milk, meat, fruits, vegetables and fish can be converted into higher value form and can save the producers from spoilage and low price. The necessity for processing at cooperative level can arise particularly in the marketing of perishable produces if the distance to the market requires long periods of transit.
2. ***Oversupply:*** Some of the commodities, like vegetables, fruits, and milk will have oversupply during certain seasons. During such periods, the surplus could be processed. If seasonable oversupply creates the need for an extended storage period, or if the available storage facilities cannot cope with current deliveries.
3. ***Middlemen exploitation:*** In every field of agricultural activities, middlemen are there. They are prevalent in agricultural credit, agricultural marketing, agricultural processing, and other agricultural activities. Efforts to free the farmers from the exploitation of middlemen is inevitable in agriculture. The monopoly of the middlemen could be broken by the cooperatives.
4. ***Stabilized income for the farmers:*** Agricultural production is seasonal in nature and farmers get income only during the harvest. Cooperative processing can attempt to stabilize the income of the farmers both in the short run and long run.
5. ***Job creation:*** Cooperative processing creates full employment opportunity both to the members and the member's family. In the factory, lot of skilled and unskilled workers can be given employment.

## Factors for the Organization of Processing Cooperatives

Processing cooperatives are not that much easier to organize. Lots of procedural activities are involved in establishing them. Their success, to a greater extent depends on nature. If monsoon fails or crop is damaged, it affects these units directly. Before organizing a processing unit the following aspects must be considered.

1. ***Place:*** The place where the unit is to be organized must be nearer to the raw material area. Processing cooperatives can be organized at woreda level and the location can be in the center of the raw material area.
2. ***Size:*** The size of the unit, capital involved, and machineries needed must be decided. These things could be decided by the members and the number of producers promoting the cooperatives as members. Members should contribute to the working capital and the long-term capital can be borrowed from financial institutions.
3. ***Feasibility:*** A feasibility study must be conducted. The study must assess:
   - *(a)* The suitability of the product for processing and the economic prospects of the industry.
   - *(b)* The price of raw material and the selling price of the product.
   - *(c)* The size and location of the industry.
   - *(d)* The cost of the project and the unit cost (fixed capital and working capital).
   - *(e)* The process of production.
   - *(f)* Assurance of continuous supply of raw material.
   - *(g)* Manpower needs.
   - *(h)* Transport arrangements.
   - *(i)* Distribution arrangements.
   - *(j)* Capacity utilization.
   - *(k)* Profitability of the investment.

4. ***Promotional agencies:*** The help of the promotional agencies for finance, marketing, technical assistance, etc. must be considered. Banking institutions must help the processing cooperatives by way of short-term and long-term loans. The capital that could be mobilized from the members can be used as short-term/working capital. The long-term loan can be issued by specialized institutions like industrial banks, government agencies, etc. For marketing or selling the finished products cooperative processing can link with consumer cooperatives and cooperative supermarkets.
5. ***Technology:*** The technology to be used for the processing must be decided. There are three types of technologies, namely indigenous technology, intermediate technology, and latest technology. Cooperative processing units can go for intermediate technology or latest technology. But latest technology is costlier.
6. ***Finance:*** A part of the financial needs of the unit must be met from the members out of their share capital contribution. The rest of the finance can be arranged through financial institutions.
7. ***Personnel:*** The type of personnel needed, both skilled and unskilled must be decided. A permanent recruiting system, training system, and welfare system must be planned.
8. ***Time scheduled:*** The gestation period of the unit is another consideration. Gestation period means the time taken to install the machineries and start production. The time schedule to erect the unit must be strictly followed. Any delay in erecting the machines and starting the work will lead to additional expenditure.
9. ***Infrastructure:*** Getting other infrastructure facilities like, power, transport, communication, finance, machineries, etc must be considered. It is the duty of the federal and regional governments to provide the above infrastructure facilities. Before starting a processing unit, the promoters must weigh these facilities.

10. *Government Policies:* Government regulations, licensing policies, tax concessions, subsidies, market regulations, etc. must be considered properly. In developing countries governments are giving concessions to cooperatives in licensing, marketing, price regulations, etc.

**Produces Favourable for Processing**

The following produces are favorable for processing and that could be organized by the cooperatives.

1. Produces for which there is a daily demand by the consumer, such as sugar, milk, fruit, vegetable or fish.
2. Products, which, with relatively simple treatment can, yield a much higher return, like cotton.
3. Those in respect of which transport cost can be reduced through a significant reduction in weight, for example copra produced from coconuts.

**Advantages of Processing Cooperatives**

The advantages of processing cooperatives arise on account of the following considerations:

1. *Indispensable for marketing:* Co-operative processing is an indispensable part of co-operative marketing, particularly in regard to cash crops. The price-spread between the producer and the consumers is sizeable in the case of commodities which have to be processed before they reach the consumer. Consequently, successful handling of these commodities on a co-operative basis is generally not possible, unless their processing is also undertaken by co-operative institutions.
2. *Linking credit with processing:* Linking of co-operative credit and processing is necessary. To recover the loans provided by co-operative credit institution for production of the relevant agricultural commodity. Thus, adequate development of co-operative processing appears to be a factor, which should accompany large-scale expansion of co-operative credit, particularly for cash crops.

3. ***Help to consumers, co-operative:*** Co-operative processing can play a very useful role in the functioning of consumers co-operatives. For instance, in several parts of the country the distribution of sugar, produced by co-operative sugar factories, has been entrusted to co-operative supply institutions.
4. ***Base for rural industrialization:*** Co-operative processing besides strengthening the function of agricultural credit and marketing system, will provide a wide base for rural industrialization. It has been seen that wherever in the rural areas Agricultural processing has been done; the rural economy gets immediately transformed and immensely strengthened. Larger surpluses become available for further investment and larger inputs made for technical and economic advance in both agricultural and industry.
5. ***Socio-Economic change:*** Co-operative processing industries have proved to be an effective instrument of socio-economic change of the areas in which they are located. They have created not only economic opportunities, but have helped in building a class of entrepreneurs from amongst ordinary farmers. Besides, co-operative processing accelerates the rate of capital formation in agriculture both at the production and processing stages.
6. ***Release from exploitation:*** Free themselves from exploitation by dealers, processors and middlemen.
7. ***Stability of income:*** Attempts to stabilize their income in both the short- and the long-term. The short-term incentive lay in the processing rending the produce either for a longer period of time or capable of being transported more cheaply. In this way, post-harvest price fluctuations attributable to storage and the need to transport elsewhere can be kept down; the longer term incentive, however, was that the producers, as co-operative member-owners of the processing equipment could make up for, falling prices.

8. *Improving bargaining power:* By joint processing through co-operatives of perishable produce like milk, meat, fruit, vegetables and fish, the producers can improve their negotiating position, a better price for their produce.
9. *Value addition:* Co-operative processing ensured that the added value accrued to the member-producers, where it would otherwise have passed into the hands of the various owners of the processing companies.
10. *Job creation:* Co-operative processing creates jobs, both for the other members of the farmer's family and for himself once the harvest is over.

**Feasibility Studies for Processing Cooperatives**

Feasibility studies — also termed project evaluation, pre-construction survey, etc. — are systematic appraisal of the economic and possibly social effects which the realization of a certain project will have, and a survey of the technical problems involved. Co-operatives can be confronted with the need for such an analysis, for example, if a new society or a new branch is to be established, if new activities are to be undertaken, etc. In a wider sense a similar study, though perhaps not so elaborate, should precede any decision which could decisively alter the course of a society.

In smaller matters this analysis can be prepared and assessed by the society's staff or, in the case of societies to be formed, by a pre-cooperative study group of prospective members, but in most cases a qualified economist or engineer, or both, have to be consulted. Within the co-operative sector this type of extension service can usually be contacted through central business organizations, auditing associations or government departments. In some instances feasibility studies are also carried out by international organizations involved in co-operative extension work or by private consulting firms.

In most cases the study is carried out according to a schedule similar to the following:

**1. Terms of reference**

In this preface it should be established on whose authority the study is being made, and the exact objectives it is to pursue. For the further course of the study it is important that this purpose is clearly stated. It should also include the course the study will follow and the source of information on which it will rely.

**2. Introduction**

The introduction must present the background information to the project:

*(a)* General aspects which may affect the project, such as the relevant legislation, the structure of local administration, income statistics, etc., and a general description of the area where the project will be carried out, its geographical factors, climate, communication system, people and customs. In the individual case it may also include specialized information, in rural projects, for example, about soil qualities, rainfall, land tenure and utilization, average farm size, methods of farming, etc.

*(b)* The scope for development or the need for new facilities, at present as well as in the future, by showing the faults and disadvantages of the present set-up or situation, or by proving, by way of market analysis, the room for expansion.

*(c)* The suggested target for expansion or the proposed capacity of any new facilities.

*(d)* The possible approach or method to be used and, if necessary, a comparison of several methods, and the planned location of any facilities.

*(e)* The time schedule for the realization of the project considering the recruitment and training period for any new staff, the delivery period for any new machinery and the construction time for any new buildings required as well as the most favorable time to start the project with regard to the market.

(f) The size of membership related to the set targets and the possibility of attracting new members.

(g) The expected response from present or prospective members, especially whether they realize the necessity of the project and are willing to co-operate, or what steps can be taken to enlist their collaboration.

**3. Market Analysis Research**

The key questions that should be answered in the Market Analysis section of the feasibility study are presented below:

(a) What is the current or projected demand for your proposed products or services? In other words, how many units can you reasonably expect to sell each month?

(b) What are the target markets for this product or service? What demographic characteristics do these potential customers have in common? How many of them are there?

(c) What is the projected supply in your area of the products or services needed for your project?

(d) What competition exists in this market? Can you establish a market niche, which will enable you to compete effectively with other providing this product or service?

(e) Is the location of your proposed business or project likely to affect in success? If so, is the identified site the most appropriate one available?

The market analysis should be conducted first because it is critical to the success of the business. If you cannot substantiate through research that adequate demand for your product or service exists, or if you cannot obtain sufficient quality to meet expected demand, then your project is not feasible. You should not continue to the next step in the feasibility study.

**4. Organizational Issues**

(a) What organizational structure is the right one for you?

(b) Who will serve on the board of directors?

(*c*) What qualifications are needed to manage this business?

(*d*) Who will manage the business (if possible)?

(*e*) What other staffing needs does the co-op have? How do you expect staffing needs to change over the next 2 – 3 years?

**5. Technical requirements**

(*a*) The feasibility of using the existing facilities and the present staff for the new task and the possible changes to be made for their adaptation.

(*b*) Any new facilities and manpower needed and their availability:

(*i*) Land and buildings, their size, design, outlay and equipment.

(*ii*) Machinery, type, make, capacity.

(*iii*) Transport, type, capacity.

(*iv*) Manpower, required skill and experience, recruitment plan.

Key questions to answer

(*a*) What are the technology needs for the proposed business?

(*b*) What other equipment does your proposed business need?

(*c*) Where from will you obtain this technology and equipment?

(*d*) When can you get the necessary equipment?

(*e*) How much will the equipment and technology cost?

**6. Capital outlay and finance**

(*a*) The total cost of the project assessed according to a detailed list of the costs of any building, machinery or vehicles needed and, if possible, accompanied by tenders of the relevant suppliers.

(*b*) The required rate of finance calculated on the basis of the expected average lifetime of the invested assets.

(*c*) The source of finance available for the purpose of the project.

Financial aspects to be considered

(a) ***Start-up costs:*** These are the costs incurred in starting up a new business, including "capital goods" such as land, buildings, equipment, etc. The business may have to borrow money from a lending institution to cover these costs.

(b) ***Operating costs:*** These are the ongoing costs, such as rent, utilities, and wages that are incurred in the everyday operation of a business. The total should include interest and principle payments on any debt for start-up costs.

(c) ***Revenue projections:*** How will you price your goods or services? Assess what the estimated monthly revenue will be.

(d) ***Sources of financing:*** If your proposed business will need to borrow money from a bank or other lending institution, you may need to research potential lending sources.

(e) ***Profitability analysis:*** This is the "bottom line" for the proposed business. Given the costs and revenue analysis above, will your business bring in enough revenue to cover operating expenses? Will it break even, lose money or make a profit? Is there anything you can do to improve the bottom line?

7. **Analysis of operating costs** (salary, taxes, interest, etc.)

(a) The breakdown of the expected operating cost including the proportional overhead expenses calculated for various levels of output or development:

   (i) based pm estimated costs.

   (ii) by comparison with a society which has already carried out a similar project taking into account the cost variations caused by differences in size, location, structure of membership and efficiency in management.

(b) The comparison of differing methods with respect to operating costs.

**8. Analysis of expected benefits**

The assessment of added revenue gained from the project or of the expected decrease in cost or improvement in service.

**9. Final Assessment**

(a) The comparison of the increased operating cost with the additional revenue expected (break-even graph).

(b) The influence of the new project on the overall profitability of the society.

(c) The reasons which would make the project feasible despite a decrease in profitability, for instance, the long-term effect on the development of the society.

**10. Appendix**

The appendix should include all those documents, statistics, tenders, drawings to which the text of the feasibility study refers.

A MODEL FEASIBILITY STUDY
(THIS MAY BE HELPFUL TO YOU IN FUTURE)

*Study of the possibilities of expanding a co-operative processing society*

1. What is the present economic situation of the society?
   (a) area of operation, membership.
   (b) Activities, turnover.
   (c) Management and staff.
   (d) Balance sheet and other records.
2. Is there scope for an expansion of the established activities?
   (a) by increasing the membership:
      - Are there farmers in the area of operation who are eligible for membership but who are not yet members?
      - What is the degree of competition from other marketing institutions in the area?

- What can the society do to attract these farmers despite competition? Can it improve services or give better prices?

(*b*) by increasing the area of operation:

- Are there co-operative processing societies already working in adjoining areas? If so, is an amalgamation feasible or possible?
- What other marketing institutions have established themselves in the adjoining areas, and could the society compete with them?
- What effect would the increased average distance between member and society have on the marketing costs?

(*c*) by increasing the turnover per member:

- Are the present members completely loyal to the society? If not, what can be done to improve this situation? Does the possibility of introducing delivery contracts exist?
- Can the society initiate a scheme by which the members increase their production, e.g. new farming methods?

3. Is an expansion along the current lines desirable? Can the market absorb more produce without a significant fall in price?
4. Is there scope for expansion by taking up new activities?

(*a*) by marketing other farming products not yet covered?

- What other crop or animal product is produced in the area in sufficient quantity to give a basis for organized marketing?
- For which of these products is there a suitable market?
- What competition would the society have to face in this field?

(b) by taking up other activities such as credit, supply, or other services:

- For which of these activities is there a sufficient demand among members or prospective members?
- What competition would the society have to face in any of these fields?

5. Would the society be able to cope with an expansion in connection with:

(a) top management?

- Is the present management capable of taking on additional functions? If not, are there suitable facilities for further training? And would the present management be able and willing to undergo such training?
- Is the present management willing to shoulder new responsibilities? If not, would an increase in salary act as an incentive?
- Would it be possible and feasible to replace the present management with more experienced persons?

(b) staff?

- Is the present staff adequate in quantity and quality to cope up with an increase in work and duties?
- Are there staff training facilities?
- Can the society recruit additional experienced staff?

(c) facilities?

- Are the present facilities of the society adequate for additional functions with regard to space, equipment and transport?
- What new investments would be necessary? And what would be the cost?

- What are the possibilities of securing the necessary finance?
- What sources are available?

6. How would the increased costs compare with the additional revenue? Is the overall profitability of the society maintained, increased, decreased or endangered?

**Merits of Feasibility Studies to Processing Cooperatives**

1. Whenever a new cooperative is to be organized, the scope for the viability and survival of such cooperative can be predicted. Through the feasibility studies, we can come to know the strength and weakness of such proposed processing cooperatives.
2. These are the days where cooperatives expand their businesses, open new offices and branches. Whenever cooperatives open new branches or offices, the success of such new units could be predicted accurately by cooperatives.
3. In raising deposits and mobilizing resources, feasibility studies can help the cooperatives by suggesting new methods and measures. Because resource mobilization for a new processing cooperative will decide the financial strength of the cooperative.
4. Sick units and dormant cooperatives can be revived by using feasibility studies. When a cooperative processing is unable to function properly, through feasibility studies we can improve its working conditions.
5. Cooperatives work under competition. Competition comes mainly from the private sector. Private sector is well established in processing sector and to defeat them in the competition is a tough task. What type of competition they face could be ascertained by feasibility studies.
6. The produces manufactured by the processing cooperatives are the essential commodities in the daily life of the consumers. Such consumers are poorer sections

of the community and middle class. The relations of the consumers and the members of cooperatives could be examined by this method. Their problems could also be solved.

7. Governments are entrusted in promoting industries to stop import of commodities and avoid shortages of goods. Governments use to identify such areas for industrial promotion. Reactions and attitudes of Government towards their co-operatives could be predicted by this method of research.
8. Whenever cooperatives introduce new products the success of such new products can be predicted by this method.
9. The market share of bigger cooperatives can be surveyed and steps can be suggested to increase the market share in future, by this research.

**Business Plan Outline for Processing Cooperatives**

**I. Description of the Cooperative**

Under the title description of the cooperative, we have to discuss the nature of the business, location of the business, the competitors, competencies, etc.

*Nature of the Business*

1. The type of products and services to be dealt with (milk, milk products, vegetables, fruits, processed foods, etc.).
2. Organisational description of the cooperative (how to organize, when to organize, composition of the members, etc.).

*Location of the Business*

1. Name the proposed head quarters for the cooperative.
2. Examine the transport, communication facilities available to the members.

3. The number of households in the proposed area of operation.
4. Approximate households to be absorbed as members and their background, and economic potential.
5. The sustainability of the membership-target to increase the membership every year.
6. The number of dairy animals owned and the expected supply of milk to the cooperative.
7. The type of vegetables/fruits grown and the expected supply.

*The competitors*

1. Examine the type of competition that may come once the cooperative is started.
2. Form strategies to face the competition.
3. Examine the role and stake of the prospective members and directors to face the competition.
4. How far the price mechanism can be used as an instrument to resist the competition.

*Competencies*

1. Geographic location — Ideal location for the vast majority of the members in terms of transport, communication, accessibility, all season mobility, etc.
2. Superior customer satisfaction — to attend to the needs of the consumers and the grievances of the consumers.
3. Form a mechanism to attend the daily problems and grievances of the customers.
4. Try to enlist as much institutional customers as possible.
5. Dedicated personnel - Recruiting the talents locally available.

## II. Organizational Analysis

The organizational analysis consists of selection/election of competent and dedicated committee members/board of directors, manager, and staff.

*Committee members*

1. Even during the preliminary stage, locate educated, dedicated and competent committee members.
2. Short training programme can be arranged for them as well as for the prospective members about the business plan.
3. The committee members must be educated about the competitive nature of the business, using of price and dividend mechanism to enlist the permanent loyalty of the members.
4. To work for the viability and sustainability of the cooperative by means of enrolling more and more members on a timeframe basis.
5. To conduct the committee meeting and general assembly meetings periodically and to introduce transparency in the operations of the cooperative.
6. Exposure visits to the committee members can be arranged at frequent intervals.

*Manager and Staff*

1. To go for a qualified manager, if available in and around the particular location
2. From the beginning he must be paid reasonable salary with adequate perquisites (fringe benefits).
3. Select adequate staff to work for the services of the members and for the faster growth of the cooperative.
4. Selfless service must be expected from the employees.
5. Training programme for the manager and the staff must be made a continuous process.
6. Exposure visits to the staff can be arranged at frequent intervals.

## III. Marketing and Sales Analysis

*Overall marketing strategy*

1. Marketing penetrating strategy

2. Growth strategy (monthwise and yearwise).

*Procurement strategy*

1. Procurement timings every day.
2. Fixation of procurement responsibility to each staff
3. Purchasing/procurement target.
4. Storage facility.
5. Preservation facility.
6. Steps to avoid wastage, pilferage during procurement stage and storage stage.

*Pricing Strategy*

1. Study the market price for the intended produces.
2. Try to fix a price slightly above the market price.
3. If possible, from the beginning create a price fluctuation fund, from out of the net profit, to offset the down fall in market price.

*Sales strategy*

1. Identify institutional customers (Institutional customers are bulk purchasers and payment will not be a problem).
2. Timeliness and speed of the sales very important.
3. The sales force (employees) must be motivated to take care of the quality, timeliness, cleanliness, etc., of providing supplies.

*Transport and communication services*

1. To start with higher private transport services.
2. The transport system must cover nearest cities, and institutional and individual customers.
3. Alternative arrangements to be made if regular transport service is disrupted.
4. Any transport dislocation should be communicated to the customers immediately.
5. The sales staff must be provided with communication facilities.

6. The head office and manager must be provided with round the clock communication facilities (mobile phone).

## IV. Financial Analysis

The cooperative needs two types of capital viz., block capital (long term capital) and working capital. Block capital is needed to construct office buildings, purchase equipment, etc. Working capital is needed to meet the day-to-day expenses and monthly establishment expenditures.

*Members stake*

1. To start with members may contribute very little amount as share capital. But minimum shares to be taken and value of each share can be fixed.
2. From out of the business dealings, members can be asked to contribute compulsory savings.
3. Voluntary savings can also be opened to the members.

*Voluntary agencies*

1. Voluntary agencies like the NGOs can be approached to contribute towards the funds by way of revolving fund, etc.
2. Voluntary agencies can be approached to provide equipment and furniture.

*Government*

1. Government can be approached to provide block capital (repayable long-term loan, as being practiced in many developing countries).
2. Government can provide subsidies for the purchase of equipment.
3. Government can provide tax exemptions and duty exemptions while import of equipment.

*Commercial banks*

1. Commercial banks can be approached for raising block capital and working capital.

### V. Cost and Profitability Analysis

1. *Break-even Analysis:* The proposed cooperative must be able to earn a profit at the end of third year. Strategies must be worked out.
2. *Cost Analysis:* Cost must be worked out in terms of fixed cost and variable cost. Flexibility must be allowed in the case of variable cost to attain profitability at the end of third year. To keep the cost to the minimum, the cooperative can go for rented building, hired vehicles, etc. during the beginning years.
3. *Profit Analysis:* The proposed cooperative should give a reasonable dividend and not a high dividend. A ceiling of 25 per cent can be fixed.
4. *Reserves and retained earnings:* Every year from the net profit reserves must be created. A percentage of retained earnings (e.g. 25%) must be created to plough back the profit money to the business.

## Defects, Difficulties, and Suggestions for Processing Cooperatives

One very important problem facing the cooperative processing is the problem of under-utilization of their installed capacity. Some of the problems, which the processing societies are facing, are as under:

1. ***Inadequate supply:*** Some of the processing societies especially rice mills could not work to their full installed capacities because of inadequate supply of raw materials.
2. ***Price fluctuations:*** Hazards arising out of price fluctuations and market competition have also stood in the way of maximum utilization of the installed capacity of processing societies.
3. ***Inadequate working capital:*** Modern processing units require huge capital. The members of the cooperative being marginal, small growers have not been able to contribute enough finance. This lack of adequate working capital has retarded the growth and development of cooperative processing societies.

4. ***Lack of suitable managerial personnel:*** The successful planning, installation, and functioning of a processing unit will largely depend on the caliber and competence of suitable managerial personnel, especially the chief executive officer of the unit. The working of some of the cooperative processing units has suffered on account of lack of suitable trained managerial personnel.
5. ***Time-lag in installation:*** The progress of cooperative processing units has also been hampered on account of too much time taken in the installation of the factory, mill, or any other plant. On account of too much time-lag in installation, it becomes difficult to keep alive interest and confidence of its members.
6. ***Domination of traders:*** A cooperative processing society is expected to be established and owned by the primary producers. Some of the processing units were however, dominated by the traders.
7. ***Lack of cost consciousness:*** Many of the cooperative processing units have hardly realized the importance of cost consciousness, which is necessary right from the preparation of project, selection of machinery, designing, lay-out, etc. It is because of lack of cost consciousness that many processing units are running in losses.
8. ***Defective pricing policies:*** Some of the processing units have come to grief on account of defective pricing policies pursued by them in their buying and selling operations. The task of fixing correct pricing policies for processing units assumes greater significance on account of high fluctuations in the prices of raw materials specially in case of groundnut, cotton, oilseeds, etc.
9. ***Other defects:*** Some of the important factors limiting the development of processing units are as under:
   - *(i)* Inadequacy of block capital;
   - *(ii)* Delay in getting loans from financial institutions;
   - *(iii)* Lack of technical know how;

- *(iv)* Inability of members to raise the required share capital speedily;
- *(v)* Inability of units to provide margin money; and
- *(vi)* Lack of raw materials.

**Suggestions**

1. ***Proper preliminary planning***

   Before setting up a new processing unit in the cooperative sector, a proper and detailed investigation into the following aspects should invariably be undertaken:

   - *(i)* The extent of availability of agricultural produce to be processed within the area of operation of the proposed society.
   - *(ii)* The extent to which the need for the proposed processing unit is felt by the growers and the prospects of attracting their loyalty.
   - *(iii)* Examination of the estimates of recurring income and expenditure including interest and depreciation charges, so as to consider the overall economics of the proposed units.
   - *(iv)* Facilities for transport of raw material and disposal of finished products.

2. ***Pattern of organization***

   The pattern of organization has a bearing on future viability of a processing unit. An appropriate organizational pattern facilitates business operations, optimizes efficiency and reduces costs. In this connection it has been suggested that basically the processing units, not involving heavy capital outlay, should normally be set up as an adjunct to marketing cooperatives and large size processing units should be organized as independent processing units of the growers on the lines of cooperative sugar factories or cotton growers spinning mills.

3. ***Regular supply of raw materials***

   Arrangements are essential for getting regular supply of the required raw materials and proper storage of the same. The processing cooperatives should also take greater interest in the extension effort that is needed to promote the cultivation of the required crops.

4. ***Proper storage facilities***

   The processing cooperative societies are supposed to make the bulk of their purchases from growers immediately after the harvest, it is highly desirable that they make adequate arrangements for the storage of raw materials on a scale much bigger than that of the private units.

5. ***Technical know-how***

   The development of cooperative agricultural processing units needs specialized technical assistance for identification of areas, location of site, selection of plants and machinery, technical audit of the processing units in production etc. for obvious reasons, it may not be possible for the individual processing unit to secure services of specialized technical experts for this purpose. To obviate this difficulty a programme of setting up technical cell consisting of qualified engineers, technologist, processing marketing experts etc. should be introduced.

6. ***Trained and qualified staff***

   For success a processing unit will largely depend on trained and qualified staff, it is necessary that these societies have suitably technical and trained personnel and security of their tenure.

7. ***Processing of food grains***

   Cooperatives should take initiative in taking up processing of food grains particularly wheat and maize. They should be encouraged to take up processing activities in case of these commodities by installing composite flour mills, bakeries, factories for production of breakfast foods, etc.

8. ***Open market purchase***

   The cooperative mills should be persuaded to make open market purchase of paddy in sufficient quantity so as to feed the rice mills to their full capacity.

The importance of processing programme in the overall strategy of agricultural development and also as an instrument of rural industrialization and generation of employment in rural areas cannot be over-stressed. It is therefore, imperative that governments should take special interest in the development of cooperative processing units. It is imperative that adequate funds should be made available for government contributions to the share capital of these units.

**Summary**

- Processing cooperatives are one of the important segments of agricultural cooperatives. They are classified as industrial cooperatives also in some countries.
- There are certain internal and external factors that favor the processing cooperatives.
- Processing cooperatives provide value addition to the agricultural commodities and provide good income to the farmers.
- Before organizing a processing cooperative, a feasibility study must be undertaken. This study shows the scope for organizing a processing society.
- After undertaking the feasibility study, a business plan must be undertaken. A business plan is about the future business potential of a processing cooperative.

**Self-learning Activity**

Try to answer the following questions on your own:

1. Point out the significance of processing cooperatives.
2. Discuss the importance of feasibility study for organizing processing cooperatives?
3. Explain the key factors needed for the organization of processing cooperatives
4. Explain in brief the contents of a business plan.

# 4 Working Trends, Progress and Problems of Various Processing Cooperatives

## Working of Sugar Cooperatives

Sugar is one of the essential commodities of the consumers. It is being consumed by variety of ways in rural areas and urban areas. In tropical countries, sugar is manufactured using sugarcane. But in cold countries and European countries, sugar is manufactured from sugar beet, a root crop. In several countries, farmers go for manufacturing country sugar by crushing sugarcane. The method adopted is very old and crude. Lot of wastages arise through this old method. Modern days saw the organization of sugar factories, which has become an organized sector. Sugar factories have been organized in private sector, public sector and cooperative sector.

Sugar cooperatives are one of the important processing cooperatives, which may be classified as industrial cooperatives also. Sugar cooperatives are very popular in countries like India, Indonesia, and in several European countries.

## Advantages of Sugar Cooperatives

1. Sugarcane is long period crop that takes a year for yield. It is a high-income commercial crop. Sugar cooperatives can assure a good income to the farmers. Compared to the food crops, sugarcane being a commercial crop can fetch high income to the farmers.

2. For small farmers sugar cooperative provide good bargaining power. Small farmers can produce limited quantity of sugarcane. They may not have facilities to transport sugarcane and market it profitably. A cooperative sugar factory can give good bargaining power to the small farmers.
3. Through sugar cooperatives value addition is given to the farmers. Conversion of sugarcane and sugar juice into sugar is a value addition. Sugar is used as raw material for many products like alcohol, chemicals, beverages, etc. Such uses give additional importance and price to the farmers.
4. Sugar cooperatives act as growth centers in a locality and they work for the overall development of the particular location. This is possible by means of providing new employment opportunities to the skilled and unskilled manpower around the location of the sugar cooperative. The new income generated to the farmers and the people around the factory can provide good spending power. The farmers also add additional purchasing power through the sugar cooperatives. New industries and allied industries may also come around the cooperative sugar factory. This process is called as growth center.
5. Sugar cooperatives provide employment opportunity and encourage by-product development like distillery units, paper units, etc. As noted earlier, cooperative sugar factory can employ skilled and unskilled manpower and can provide employment opportunity to the local population. By means of organizing distillery units and paper units, additional employment can also be created.
6. Sugar cooperatives are also working for the principle "Concern for Community". This denotes that a cooperative should not stop serving the members alone. On the other hand, it has to serve the non-members and community through several ways. They provide facilities like educational, medical, agricultural extension, etc. They

also provide public amenities like construction of roads, rural electrification, distribution of agricultural inputs, etc. to the farmers.

7. They meet the important consumption need of the country by providing sugar at a reasonable price to consumers. In controlling the price of sugar, cooperative sugar factories balance the activities of the private sector.
8. Cooperative sugar factories can contribute to the export earnings of the country by means of exporting surplus sugar to foreign countries. Thereby, they contribute to the nations' cause of earning foreign exchange.

**Preconditions Needed for Sugar Cooperatives**

1. ***Location of the factory***
   The sugar factory should be located in a place with infrastructural facilities like road, transport, communication, etc. While a feasibility study is undertaken, this infrastructure facilities must be considered carefully.
2. ***Raw material***
   The factory should be surrounded by sugarcane cultivation area. The raw material should be of good quality. The proposed cooperative sugar factory must have tie up with agricultural research stations and extension agencies. Improved sugarcane seeds must be given to the farmers through such agencies.
3. ***Continuous supply***
   Continuous supply of raw materials is another precondition for the successful working of a cooperative sugar factory. The cooperative must plan the sugarcane cutting order properly and inform the members well in advance and fix dates for each member to bring the sugarcane to the factory.
4. ***Loyalty of the Farmers***
   The farmers should work for the success of the factory by means of providing enough sugarcane, providing capital needed and by providing good management. In

many countries when private sugar factories pay high price, the cooperative members switch their supply to the private factories. This trend should be avoided.

5. ***Technology:*** For erecting a new sugar factory, latest technology is needed, through which the cost of production can be reduced. Latest technology can be obtained from foreign countries or it can be developed indigenously.
6. ***Transport***

   The factory must arrange sound transport arrangement to transport the sugarcane from the field to the factory. One of the factors for the success of a cooperative sugar factory is the efficient transport system. Transport system is also needed to distribute the sugar to various parts of the country.
7. ***Power supply***

   The factory should be ensured uninterrupted power supply at a reasonable cost. A cooperative sugar factory being a large-scale industry consumes heavy power. Electricity can be supplied at a reduced rate to the cooperative sugar factories because they fulfill one of the nation's needs of supplying an essential consumer article for a reasonable price.
8. ***Government regulations***

   The government policies relating to licensing, price fixation, taxation, etc. should be conducive to the cooperatives. For example, in India, the government followed a licensing policy of 50-50 per cent to the cooperatives and the private sector. Governments can also provide tax concessions and excise duty concessions to the cooperative sugar factories.

**Membership**

Those farmers who are producing sugarcane can become the members of sugar cooperatives. They are expected to make initial contribution heavily to the formation of the factory. When an individual is admitted as a member of a cooperative sugar factory, they should come to an agreement with the factory to supply all the sugarcanes to the cooperative sugar factory. Many times, members divert the sugarcane for the private sugar factories. When evidence is produced such members are removed from the membership of the cooperative sugar cooperative.

**Capital**

A sugar cooperative is in need of two types of capital.

1. Block Capital or Fixed Capital
2. Working Capital

*Block Capital*

Heavy block capital for a sugar cooperative is needed to purchase land, to purchase machineries, and to construct buildings. Members cannot contribute the block capital needs. On the other hand sugar cooperatives can borrow these heavy amounts from industrial banks, foreign banks, etc.

*Working Capital*

Working capital is needed to meet the current expenditures of the sugar cooperative. Members' contribution of share capital can be used for the working capital purpose. In certain cases, sugar cooperatives also lend money for the farmers for the purchase of improved sugarcane seeds, fertilizers, etc. The money is collected during the sale of the sugarcane to the factory.

**Mode of Business**

Sugar cooperatives come to an agreement with each member to supply sugarcane of certain hectares. The farmer has to inform the cooperative about the maturity period and the factory will order for sugarcane cutting. After receiving the sugarcane cutting order the farmer will arrange to cut the sugarcane on his own expense and ask for transport arrangement. In certain cases the farmers have to make their own transport arrangements. After the sugarcane delivery is made, the farmer will be paid the money as per the prevailing price fixed either by the government or by the market. When a farmer has borrowed loan, the loan amount will be deducted from the final settlement.

**Management**

Cooperative sugar factories are managed like any other cooperative organization. But the board should consist of people who have vast knowledge and experience in the field of agriculture and manufacturing. They should also have the knowledge of business to sell the sugar and sugar-related products for a profitable price. They should also give leadership for ancillary production and expansion of the sugar cooperative.

**Rural Entrepreneurs**

One of the most important contributions of co-operative sugar factories has been that they are increasingly becoming focal points for development of agro-industrial complexes in the rural areas. The Sugar Enquiry Commission of India has observed:

> "the setting up of a co-operative sugar factory has acted as a nucleus for social and economic development of the area around it and has helped to develop a new class of rural entrepreneurs". Many of them have undertaken development of by-products industries like alcohol, pharmaceuticals and paper projects, and have became the nucleus of development of other co-operative development activities like poultry, piggeries, lift irrigation schemes, solvent extraction plants and many others.

Alongside the welfare of the grower-members, the co-operatives have shown a keen interest in the welfare of the workers and the community, etc., and have contributed largely to the coming into being of township with schools, colleges, polytechnics, hospitals, places of worship, centers for cultural and social activities, etc., in the sugar factory areas.

Sugar co-operatives have afforded a unique opportunity to the small sugarcane cultivator to take full benefits of large-scale management and organization. Wherever co-operative sugar factories have been successfully established, they have proved instruments of development. Being decentralized processing units of small cultivators, sugar cooperatives are serving as effective agencies in the diffusions of benefits of development plans in an even manner and helping in the fulfillment of the concept of socialist pattern of society. One of the most significant benefits of co-operative sugar factories has been the spirit of self-reliance generated amongst small growers.

**Linking with Consumer Cooperatives**

For the effective distribution of sugar and to help the common man, the sugar cooperatives must have a link with the consumer cooperatives. They can supply the sugar to the Regional Consumer Cooperative Federations or to the cooperative wholesale stores. These apex institutions can distribute the sugar through the primary consumer cooperatives and cooperative supermarkets. During certain seasons, shortage may arise in the supply of sugar. During such times, the consumer should be put to lot of difficulties and the private merchants exploit them charging higher prices. Consumer cooperatives can avoid shortage and price rise of sugar.

**Problems of Sugar Co-operatives**

Throughout the post-war period, the price of sugar has been established as a result of government policy and has been foxed at levels relatively profitable. The grower of sugarcane, who is a member of co-operative sugar factory, has thus profited from stabilized prices. No problems of sale and distribution in the disposal of sugar have arisen during these years. Therefore, the running of a sugar factory has presented chiefly problems of production, rather than of sale of the end-products.

1. The most important problem, which has confronted the sugar co-operatives, is the problem of under-utilization of their installed capacities. The main factors responsible for under-utilization are:
   *(i)* Shortage of sugarcane;
   *(ii)* Diversions of sugarcane for manufacture of country sugar;
   *(iii)* Working hours lost due to stoppages;
   *(iv)* Inadequacy of early and late maturing varieties of sugarcane in the factory zone.
2. Adequate and regular supply of good quality sugarcane is an important prerequisite for improved efficiency and strengthening the economy of a sugar factory. In several cases, a private sugar factory is located near to the cooperative sugar factory. To get adequate supply of sugarcane, the private sugar factories pay higher price to the sugarcanes to divert the sugarcane from cooperative sugar factories. This is a testing circumstance for a cooperative sugar factory. Only the loyalty of the members can avoid such situations.
3. An important source of capital accumulation in a co-operative sugar factory is the collection of non-refundable deposit from the sugarcane price payable to members. It is observed that a number of co-operatives are not regular in the collection of this amount. Consequently, the share capital base has not been strengthened to the desired extent. The failure to enforce compulsory deductions from sugarcane price is often attributed to competition from other sweetening agents and unwillingness of the members to agree to deductions. Efforts to collect non-refundable deposits need not be slackened.
4. The profitable utilization of the important by-products of sugar namely molasses and bagasse, continue to be a serious problem facing the co-operative sugar factories. The molasses and bagasse in stock are generally in huge quantity and are even deteriorating. Sugar factories may,

therefore, be enabled to establish alcohol plants, hard-board and chipboard factories, paper plants, etc. Government may help in the preparation of project reports and in the organization of such by-product industries.

5. Cooperative sugar factories are in need of huge working capital and block capital. Working capital is needed to pay the farmers the sugarcane price immediately. Block capital or long-term capital is needed to purchase equipments, machineries, and replace old machineries. Such long-term capital should be available for a long period at a low rate of interest. Separate long-term institutional financing system must prevail in a country.
6. One of the major problems of the cooperative sugar factories is that they are unable to pay the sugarcane price properly and in time to the farmers. In several developing countries, cooperative sugar factories have kept the payment arrears for two or three years. This makes the farmers a distrust to the cooperative sugar factories and they divert their sugarcane to private sugar factories, who are very prompt in the payment of money to the farmers.

### Scope for the Organization of Sugar Cooperative in Ethiopia

Ethiopia, being an agricultural country, has enormous scope for organizing cooperative sugar factories. One of the preconditions to organize cooperative sugar factories is to construct irrigation dams and provide assured irrigation facilities to the farmers. Because sugarcane is a crop, which needs irrigation throughout the year. Here below, find the discussion on the scope for organizing sugar cooperatives in Ethiopia.

1. The country has good fertile soil and climate for the cultivation of sugarcane. Black soil is most suitable soil for the cultivation of sugarcane. The fertility of the soil in Ethiopia is very high compared to other African countries.

2. Good rainfall is a positive factor. In highland areas and in several parts of lowland areas, good rainfall takes place continuously for four or five months in Ethiopia. Sugarcane consumes lot of water and rainwater can be harvested and used for this crop.
3. At present, very few private sugar factories are manufacturing sugar in Ethiopia. They hike the price artificially during several times. The private sugar factories price mechanism can be balanced by the cooperative sugar factories, the example has been shown in India where the cooperative sugar factories produce 50 per cent of the nation's sugar production.
4. There is good demand for sugar within the country. The growth of population is steady in Ethiopia. With the growth of population and increase in income and purchasing power of the population, the demand for sugar will be growing steadily. Further, raw material, many of the industries like chocolate industry, ice-cream industry, breweries, chemical industries, etc. area.
5. Ethiopia needs fast industrialization to reduce the pressure on agriculture. A section of the population depending on agriculture must be diverted to industrial occupations. Sugar cooperatives can offer employment opportunities directly and its allied industries like breweries, paper industries, etc. can provide further employment opportunities.
6. An export opportunity for sugar is bright. During several times, Ethiopia used to import sugar from foreign countries. This trend can be changed by organizing number of cooperative sugar factories. Sugar has regular export market. With lower cost of production, the sugar that could be produced by cooperative sugar factories can be exported competitively.
7. Government support can also be expected for licensing, capital formation, etc. The present democratic government is very favorable to the cooperative

movement in Ethiopia. The government will certainly help the farmers to promote cooperative sugar factories.

8. Foreign private capital or cooperative capital can be invited to meet the financial needs of sugar cooperatives in Ethiopia. These are the days of economic liberalization. Cooperative sugar factories can have tie up with foreign private investment. Another alternative is that the capital can be mobilized from the cooperatively advanced countries like Sweden, Denmark, Ireland, Germany, etc.

**Fruit and Vegetable Processing Cooperatives**

The cooperative processing of perishable products like fruit and vegetable involves considerably high risks than marketing and processing of other crops, especially if the marketing is not confined to daily sales on local markets that require delivery to distant markets. Societies taking up these activities need experienced and well-trained management and sound financial resources.

**Peculiarities of Fruit and Vegetable Processing Cooperatives**

Such cooperatives are rare and they are coming under processing cooperatives. The peculiarities of such cooperatives are as follows:

1. *Deal with perishable commodities:* The specialty of the fruit and vegetable-processing cooperatives is to deal with agricultural produces, mainly perishable in nature. The life of such commodities are shorter and within the short period they must be sold or converted into different form like fruit juices, jam, or canned food.

2. *Supply of raw material:* Like other agricultural commodities, the supply of fruits and vegetables are seasonal in nature. When supply is higher than demand, the farmers will be affected by getting lower price. Such trend could be avoided by means of taking the surplus produces for processing activities.

3. *High dependence on nature:* Dependence on nature to produce these commodities is high. Fruits and vegetables

are prone to whether conditions, rainfall, climatic conditions, etc. Even the pest attack is high for such commodities than for cereal crops.

4. *Modern technology:* Modern technology is needed for preserving, storing, and manufacturing activities. Without using modern technology, a processing unit cannot be run successfully. Even by using intermediate or indigenous technology, storing and preserving can be undertaken, but they cannot be effective for large-scale operations. Technology is also needed for various stages of manufacturing activities and conversion processes.
5. *Brand name:* A brand name is needed to sell the finished products. The private sector and multi-nationals are able to shine in this sector out of the creation of brand name. So, cooperatives must also go for brand names. In America, brand name such as Sunkist for citrus, Land O Lake for dairy and poultry products, Welch for grape juices, and Diamond for walnuts are used. In India, Amul is a popular brand name for cooperative dairy products. In Denmark, Lurbrand is a trademark for cooperative dairy products. Through brand name, the cooperatives can compete with the private sector and they can capture internal market and export market.
6. *Marketing network:* A good marketing outlet is necessary to sell the products. So enough promotional measures should be undertaken. Fruits and vegetables are perishable items and as such they are handled mainly by the private traders. Private traders have good marketing network among themselves. So for the processing cooperatives to undertake such marketing network is a serious problem. For the promotional measures, huge money must be spent on advertisement. This cost must be borne by the cooperatives.
7. *Export market:* An export market is desirable for such cooperatives. Fruit and vegetable processing cooperatives should not depend only on local market. On the other

hand, they must take efforts to export their products to foreign countries. As the products would be costlier in the home country for the ordinary citizens, export avenue can balance the business transaction of the processing cooperatives.

8. *Finance:* Heavy capital will be involved for organizing such cooperatives. Processing cooperatives like other industrial cooperatives are in need of huge amount of fixed capital or block capital. This capital cannot be mobilized from the members. On the other hand, they have to look after the industrial banks, cooperative banks, or commercial banks. Heavy capital is needed to purchase land and construct the buildings, capital is also needed to purchase technology, equipment, and machineries. As wear and tear would be high in these industries, replacement of machineries and spare parts must be done at a reasonable periods. Otherwise, it may lead to stoppage of work and production.
9. *Members loyalty:* The loyalty of the members for continuous supply of quality raw material are very much needed. The members of such cooperatives usually have the attitude of selling the poor quality produces to the cooperatives and the good quality produces in the open market for a higher price. This attitude must be changed and the members must continuously supply quality produces to the cooperatives.
10. *Competing ability:* Such cooperatives have to compete with well-organized private sector and MNCs. In the field of fruit and vegetable processing private sector and multi-national corporation have strong hold. For quite a long time, they have vast experiences in this field and they have specialized in technology, production, marketing, and promotion. Many MNCs have widespread hold over specified products throughout the world. So, to compete them is a challenging task.

11. *Capacity utilization:* The processing cooperatives have to take care of the fuller utilization of the installed capacity. Continuous supply of quality raw materials is a precondition for such capacity utilization. Stoppage of work due to power shortage, transport difficulties, labour problems, etc. must be avoided.

**Risks Involved in Fruit and Vegetable Processing Cooperatives**

1. The period available to transport or transform these materials without any spoilage is very short. Any delay in transport through traffic congestion, breakdowns, customs controls, etc. can result in damage to the produce.
2. Any attempt to extend the marketing period by cold storage, deep freezing, refrigerated transport, treatment with chemicals, etc or to speed up the transport by using air transport requires high investments and expenditures and can lead to a steep increase in marketing costs. The feasibility of taking such a step depends largely on the relationship between the increased cost and the additional revenue expected from the sale of the produce and on the possibility of reimbursing any excess cost by paying less to the producer.
3. The delicate nature of the produce, which makes handling and packaging a difficult task that requires great care, skilled staff, and special packing material. In transporting these products, strong packing material is needed. On the other hand, such packing material must be durable and should not add weight to the product. The character of most fruits and vegetables as luxury rather than basic food, which makes them more dependent on changes in the consumers' preference and their purchasing power.

**Reducing the Risks**

Above risks can be averted through the following measures:

1. If the buyer could take the transport risk or if the society has enough processing facilities, the risk could be avoided.

2. The members of fruit and vegetable cooperatives have the feeling that the processing cooperative is the dumping ground to sell the poor quality produces. On the other hand, they sell quality produces to the private traders in the open market. This attitude must be changed for the successful running of the processing cooperatives.
3. Latest technology or affordable technology must be applied to the processing cooperatives. This can ensure the fuller capacity utilization of the unit and could render affordable volume of business.
4. Processing cooperatives of this type needs lot of working capital and long-term capital. Working capital can be increased stage by stage from the members and by taking a part of the profit to the working capital. But long-term capital can be arranged through industrial banks and commercial banks.
5. As the products of fruit and vegetable processing cooperatives have very good demand in export market, a tie up can be arranged with other countries' consumers cooperatives and marketing cooperatives. For example, the National Consumer Federation of Sweden (KF) imports lot of cooperative products. Likewise, the cooperative wholesale store of England can also help the import of the products of cooperatives.

The management and working of fruit and vegetable processing cooperatives are the same as other processing cooperatives. In Ethiopia there is enormous scope for the organization of such cooperatives.

## Scope for Organizing Fruit and Vegetable Processing Cooperatives in Ethiopia

1. The soil and climatic conditions are very favorable for the cultivation of abundant fruits and vegetables in Ethiopia.
2. Surplus production arises during several times. During such times lot of fruits and vegetables are sold for a lower

price by the farmers. Processing cooperatives can change the situation and can provide stable price to the farmers.

3. Majority of the farmers in Ethiopia are small farmers and many of them cultivate fruits and vegetables. A stable income can be given to them by the processing cooperatives.
4. Many African countries like South Africa and Kenya have organized processing cooperatives and export fruit juices, canned foods and processed vegetables to foreign countries. By organizing processing cooperatives, Ethiopian farmers can also export such commodities.
5. One of the preconditions needed to organize processing cooperatives is the construction of modern godowns and refrigerated system. Government can come forward to arrange these facilities to the fruit and vegetable processing cooperatives.

## Meat and Egg Processing Cooperatives

### *Significance*

One of the contributions of Danish cooperative movement is the organization of meat and egg processing cooperatives. After the successful venture of organizing dairy cooperatives, the Danish farmers ventured to start meat and egg processing cooperatives. The diversion of wheat as cattle and poultry feed led to the prospects of developing meat and poultry industry. As Denmark is popular for single-purpose cooperatives, they have started meat processing cooperatives and egg processing cooperatives successfully. This experiment has been successfully followed by Irish, New Zeland, German and Dutch farmers. In South American countries, these processing cooperatives are very popular. The following are the significance of meat and egg processing cooperatives.

1. *Cattle development:* In many developing countries of Africa, South America and Asia, cattle population is very vast and there is scope for processing this wealth.

2. *Nutrition:* Egg is a nutritious food for all age group like milk. Intake of egg and egg products is increasing in all countries year after year.
3. *By-products:* Number of byproducts like skin, bones, leather, etc are derived from cattle. Specialized industries for these byproducts can be organized.
4. *Technology:* For the scientific development of cattle and poultry population, modern technology must be planned in the fields of breeding, feeding, and disease prevention.
5. *Disease:* Cattle and poultry are susceptible to diseases like Runderpest, yellow fever, bird fever, etc. For the past few years poultry birds have been affected by bird fever in several countries. Consumption of meat or poultry, which are affected by diseases, will be harmful to human beings.

**Advantages of Meat and Egg Processing Cooperatives**

Meat and egg processing cooperatives provide the following advantages to the members, to the community, and to the nation.

1. *Additional source of income:* Cattle and poultry wealth are additional source of income to the farmers. In several countries, where pastoralism is practiced, the main occupation of the population is rearing of cattle. Cattle provide the major income for such population.
2. *Use of locally available resources:* For feeding cattle and poultry, farmers use locally available resources like grazing lands, hay from harvested crops, wasted grain, etc. Such agricultural residues will otherwise go waste. Farmers need not spend any additional money for feeding.
3. *Natural manure:* Cow dung and poultry waste are the best natural manure, which can keep the fertility of soil forever. Now-a-days, due to shortage of natural manure, farmers go for application of chemical fertilizers, which are very harmful to the soil. Even big farmers, having large size of lands can supplement chemical fertilizers with natural manure.

4. *Industrialization:* Meat and egg processing cooperatives faster the speed of industrialization. They are organized as small and medium industries and in due course they expand fast. Allied industries using cattle bone (a raw material for fertilizer units) can also be organized.
5. *Employment opportunity:* In developing countries, cattle and poultry rearing provides very good employment opportunity to the farmers. Cooperative processing units also provide employment opportunities to the skilled and unskilled people in the local area.
6. *Export opportunities:* The products of meat and egg processing cooperatives have enormous export market. The Danish cooperatives have shown to the world the value of such cooperatives in the field of export marketing.
7. *Revenue to the government:* Processing cooperatives in the field of meat and egg provide substantial income to the government by way of paying various types of taxes. They also fetch valuable foreign exchange needed for the country. For example, in Ethiopia, meat export and skin export fetches considerable foreign exchange to the country.
8. *Disease prevention:* Meat and egg processing cooperatives have appointed qualified veterinary doctors and provide veterinary services and disease prevention measures not only to members, but also to the non-members. They provide preventive medicines and injections to the cattle and poultry population. They monitor health of the cattle and forewarn the members about disease attack, disease prevention, and other precautions.
9. *Improved varieties:* Meat cooperatives introduce crossbred varieties through the measures like Artificial Insemination. They have established special laboratories to preserve the semen of improved and crossbred varieties.
10. *Environmental protection:* Meat processing is undertaken under strictly scientific environment. Governments are

very particular about the environment that could be spoiled by such industries. In the case of poultry industry, bird flu has become a threat and precaution measures are taken by the processing cooperatives to prevent such eventualities.

**Management**

Management of meat and egg processing cooperatives are the same like other processing cooperatives. While admitting new members, such cooperatives must be careful that the members have enough cattle population and poultry unit. The disloyalty of the members in the form of supplying the produced when the price in the cooperative is high, and not supplying the produces when the price is low in the cooperative should be avoided.

The board of directors or the committee members are elected regularly once in three years. Compared to other cooperatives, the management must be vigilant and cautious in running their cooperatives. Committee meetings and general assembly meetings must be held regularly as per the bylaw of cooperative.

While distributing the net profit, a percentage can be set forth for environmental control and pollution control. Because the future of such industries depends on their commitment to keep a clean environment to the society. In several countries, such processing cooperatives have been closed down due to resistance from the local population for their negligence to keep the environment clean.

**Problems and Solutions**

The meat and egg processing cooperatives face several problems, for which solutions are also given below:

1. *Competition:* Such processing cooperatives are facing competition from the private sector. Private sector in these industries has long-standing record of service. They have developed internal and external markets for a very long

time. So, cooperatives have to face competition from them by means of improving their quality and loyalty of the members.

2. *Continuous supply:* Another problem faced by such processing cooperatives is the continuous supply of quality cattle and egg. Several times egg production is affected due to diseases like bird flu. So, the cooperatives must undertake all precautionary measures to control such diseases.
3. *Veterinary services:* Many of the processing cooperatives neglect the provision of veterinary services to their members. Because, this is a specialized service, which is very costly. But neglect of veterinary service will bring down the quality of the cattle and products. The processing cooperatives can approach the government department to locate the veterinary hospital nearer to the processing cooperatives or while organizing a new processing cooperative, it can be located nearer to a government veterinary hospital.
4. *Disease attack:* Very often, cattle and poultry are affected by contagious diseases, which spread very fast from one country to another country. Processing cooperatives cannot be spared by such diseases. So, universal effort with the help of governments, WHO, and similar agencies must be undertaken.
5. *Technology:* Many processing cooperatives are following outmoded technology, which result in the poor quality of finished products. So, the processing cooperatives must import technology from advanced countries' processing cooperatives.
6. *Machineries:* Processing cooperatives need latest machineries for processing meat and egg. When technology is changing, improved technology demands the installation of latest machineries. Machineries are costlier and the processing cooperatives must make necessary arrangements to replace old machineries.

7. *Capital:* Meat and egg processing cooperatives need huge capital for setting the factory, purchasing technology and machineries. Many cooperatives have not modernized their factories due to lack of capital. The government and the financial agencies must come forward to finance such processing cooperatives. As an inbuilt measure, the processing cooperatives can approach the cooperative banks or public sector banks for finance.

## Conditions Favourable for Organizing Meat and Egg Processing Cooperatives in Developing Countries

Meat processing and egg processing cooperatives are prevalent in developed European countries. Many of the South American countries have organized meat processing cooperatives. In Asian countries — India, China and Japan, egg processing cooperatives are very popular. These processing cooperatives provide great employment opportunities for the farmers. Such cooperatives can be organized by group of farmers, like other processing cooperatives. But they have to follow certain precautions like disease control, environmental protection, etc. Following are certain favorable factors for organizing meat and egg processing cooperatives in developing countries including Ethiopia.

1. *Location:* The primary precondition for organizing meat and egg processing cooperative is the location. The location of the cooperative must be away from congested cities. The area must have sizeable population of cattle and poultry. These conditions are quite suitable for developing countries.

2. *Sizeable cattle and poultry pollution:* Developing countries comprising Asia, Africa and South America have sizeable population of cattle and poultry. For example, Ethiopia has the largest cattle population in Africa. But no meat processing or egg processing cooperatives exists in this country. These activities are handled by private sector. So, such countries have great scope to organize the above processing cooperatives.

3. *Income to the farmers:* Processing cooperatives in the field of meat and egg can provide supplementary income to the farmers other than agricultural income. Agricultural income is not continuous to the farmers throughout the year, but farmers can earn continuous income throughout the year through cattle rearing and poultry development.
4. *Value addition:* Such cooperatives provide value addition to the products. Instead of selling the cattle, through processing cooperatives meat can be prepared, preserved, packed, and exported. Likewise, egg can be powdered or processed and can be exported. Such conversion is called as value addition and provides good income to the farmers.
5. *Export avenue:* One of the preconditions for the success of the above cooperatives in developing countries is the creation of export market. Primary cooperatives cannot undertake such export marketing. On the other hand, primary processing cooperatives must organize National Federations and such National Federations can look after the export business.
6. *Government concessions:* In developing countries, the governments must provide certain concessions in the fields of licensing, taxation, regulations, export subsidies, etc. to the processing cooperatives. Because these processing cooperatives are earning income to the people and government, forms part of export revenue, and encourage employment opportunities. Governments must also make arrangement to provide long-term financial assistance to these cooperatives.
7. *Technical expertise:* Meat and egg processing cooperatives have to follow latest technology in processing, preserving, packaging, marketing, etc. Such technology is costlier and they have to be imported from foreign countries. The processing cooperatives can have tie up with other countries' cooperatives and can fulfill the principle of cooperation among cooperatives.

8. *Expanding market:* When the population increases the food needs of the country will also increases. Meat and egg form major part of the nutritious food item of human beings. Processed meat and egg are costlier and the population of developing countries may not have the purchasing power to absorb such products. So, naturally, the processing cooperatives have to concentrate on the export market.
9. *Quality products:* Cooperatives are meant for providing quality materials. The members of these cooperatives must make it a point to supply quality products to these processing cooperatives. They should not supply second quality products to the cooperatives.
10. *Continuous supply:* Like agricultural commodities, shortage may arise in the supply of cattle and egg to the processing cooperatives. When supply is not continuous, work stoppage will be there. To avoid such problems, the cooperatives must plan their activities properly.
11. *Skilled manpower:* Highly improved technology is adopted by such processing cooperatives. Hence, skilled manpower is necessary to run the processing cooperatives successfully and profitably. So, the processing cooperatives must pay high salary than the private sector.
12. *Training and development:* The members of the processing cooperatives and the leaders of the cooperatives must be given continuous training in rearing cattle and poultry. They must also be given training to run such complex processing cooperatives. Field visits to similar processing cooperatives within the country and exposure visits to other countries can be arranged regularly to the members and leaders.

**Summary**

- Sugar cooperatives are one of the important processing cooperatives, which help the farmers to increase their income and welfare.

- Sugar cooperatives are facing number of problems and major problem is relating to finance and the supply of raw materials. There is enormous scope for organizing sugar cooperatives in Ethiopia. Fruit and vegetable processing cooperatives are special types of processing cooperatives.
- Compared to other cooperatives, fruit and vegetable processing cooperatives face number of risk. Because, they deal with perishable commodities and they have to compete with the private sector and multinational corporations.
- Meat and egg processing cooperatives provide enormous income scope for the farmers. Ethiopia, being the country having largest number of cattle population in Africa, has enormous export market through the meat and egg processing cooperatives.

**Self-learning Activity**

Try to answer the following questions on your own:

1. How far a sugar cooperative becomes a "growth centre"?
2. What are the peculiarities of fruits and vegetable cooperatives?
3. Illustrate the advantages of meat and egg processing cooperatives.

# 5 Dairy Cooperatives

## Agriculture Allied Cooperatives

Agriculture allied cooperatives are providing supportive role to the agricultural cooperatives. Though they are not directly related to agriculture, their functioning and operations are supplementary to the functioning of agricultural cooperatives. For example, the crop and grain remains of agriculture are used as fodder and feed for dairy cooperatives and poultry cooperatives. A farmer can become member of agriculture allied or related cooperatives, as he has a right to become a member of very many agricultural cooperatives. Some of the agriculture allied cooperatives are discussed in the subsequent chapters.

## Dairy Cooperatives

Milk is an important liquid food for all ages of human being. Milk contains large amounts of essential nutrients and has been rightly recognized as nature's single most complete food. Nutritionally, milk has been defined as "the most nearly perfect food". Milk is an outstanding source of calcium and phosphorus for bones and teeth and contains number of vitamins. Milk as a food serves the purpose of the development of human being for their growth, reproduction, supply of energy, maintenance, and appetite satisfaction.

## Specific Features of Dairy Industry

1. *Milk as raw material:* Milk has become an important raw material for human consumption. Milk is basically a liquid

consisting of 90 per cent of water, which means it is a bulky and heavy commodity. It is produced on a daily basis. As a consequence, milk requires efficient transport system. Milk can be kept for few days, which means a time limit during which it must be used or processed. Milk is perishable in nature and subject to adulteration. The quality of raw material is highly dependent on farm management. So quality regulations are necessary.

2. *Socio-Economic position of dairy farmers:* Vast majority of milk producers are small-scale producers and have a weak position on the market and their supply is very limited. It gives daily income to the farmers. It is a labour-intensive industry and provides employment opportunity not only to the farmers but also to transport and processing sector. So in the rural development dairy sector plays a major role.
3. *Cooperative dairying:* In milk production cooperative dairying play a major role. According to International Dairy Federation Survey in 1984, in 21 countries, together account for 55 per cent of the world milk supply, cooperatives marketed 86 per cent of the total sales. In New Zealand and India, 90 per cent of milk is processed by dairy cooperatives.
4. *Milk is a vulnerable at the same time, expensive raw material:* Milk is used for the production of wide range of milk products and it is called as white gold. Processing industry is necessary to increase the value addition for milk. Without processing industry, milk sector cannot survive.
5. *Nutritional considerations:* Nutritional value of milk is high and of particular value when it is included in the diet of children. Even for elderly people and patients, milk is an important nutritional food.

Today, several forces like technological changes, economic liberalization and privatization have created greater influence on dairy industry.

**Importance of Dairy Cooperatives**

1. Dairy is a subsidiary occupation for farmers and has become a standard source of income for the farmers. A weekly income is provided by dairy to the farmers. In agriculture, a farmer cannot get continuous income.
2. Scattered milk producers are united under the fold of cooperatives and middlemen exploitation was avoided. This is quite relevant in the case of small farmers and agricultural labourers.
3. Dairy cooperatives have increased the quantity and quality of milk production. In many developed countries, like Denmark and Ireland, and in developing countries like India, we could find this. India became the major producer of milk in the world in 2002 only due to dairy cooperatives.
4. Scientific method of rearing dairy animals has increased productivity and yield per cow. Dairy cooperatives provide scientifically developed feeding, rearing, and health facilities.
5. Modern methods of cow protection have been popularized by dairy cooperatives. Up-to-date veterinary services have saved milk animals from traditional diseases.
6. The system of milk procurement and payment on weekend has increased the confidence of milk producers over the cooperatives.
7. Speedy transport system, chilling plants, byproduct manufacturing, etc. have given new thrust to the dairy cooperatives.
8. Urban population has been assured of continuous supply of milk by the dairy cooperatives. In many countries, regular supply of milk and milk products have been assured by the dairy cooperatives.
9. *Status of rural women:* Dairying has become an important occupation for women and income from dairy has increased their status in the rural areas.

10. *Removal of poverty:* Dairy cooperatives have wiped out poverty, unemployment, and low level of living in many developing countries. In other countries, such model can be applied to remove poverty.

**Factors Favouring Milk Production**

The following factors favor increase of milk production in developing countries, especially countries depending on agriculture.

1. *Current demand:* In many of the developing countries, the supply of milk and milk products is inadequate to meet the requirements of the country. Consequently, dairy imports for a high proportion of milk and milk products consumed in these countries. So, there is greater need to increase local milk production.
2. *Increasing population:* The current growth rate of population of developing countries is higher than developed countries. So, the per capita consumption of milk is expected to increase in future.
3. *Need for dietary improvement:* To counter malnutrition, in developing countries milk consumption must be improved especially for children.
4. *Rising economic levels:* The income level of population in developing countries is increasing, which can afford the population to consume nutritious food especially milk.
5. *Rising level of education:* In addition to the increase in economic level, the educational level of the population in developing countries is also increasing. This favors the high consumption of milk.
6. *Production potential:* Production potential for milk production is also high in developing countries. These countries have been traditionally producing milk and through modern methods and with the help of dairy cooperatives milk production and milk products can be increased.

### Suggestions for Small Milk Procedures

Modern milk producers, especially smallholders have to develop their dairy farming through the following systems.

1. *Feeding systems:* Improved feeding systems through crop residues, pastures, concentrates, and supplements can increase the milk yield.
2. *Breeding systems:* Local breeds crossed with improved breeds can improve the quality of dairy farming.
3. *Production system for fodder:* Specialist fodder producers, roadside harvesting, and communal management are needed.
4. *Stimulus for development:* Banking institutions, government organizations, aid organizations, and NGOs can participate in dairy development.
5. *Management:* Disease management, housing, feeding for production, animal health, all need special attention.
6. *Applicable technologies:* Protein feeding, urea and alkaline straw treatments, and vaccination programmes are needed.
7. *Market:* Local market, export market, supply for factories, etc must be taken care of.
8. *Processing:* Processing activities at village level, regional, and national level must be developed.
9. *Integration of dairy system:* Dairy farming must be integrated with other farming activities like mixed farming.
10. *Animal output:* Dried cow can be salvaged for meat.

### Methods of Operation

#### 1. *Procurement Operations*

The most important dairy activity is procurement of milk from the scattered milk producers. This is considered to be a primary activity of the diary cooperatives. The importance of procurement management is as follows:

(a) The annual activity of a dairy cooperative is decided on the basis of procurement management.

(b) A well arranged procurement system ensures the farmers a steady income and make them to have standard dairy operations.

(c) Procurement management is a factor that decides the distribution system. Number of outlets, channels of distribution, etc. are decided on the basis of procurement management.

(d) The operation of chilling plants, byproduct units, etc. depend on the procurement operations.

(e) Fuller capacity utilization of plant and machinery of various dairy units is decided upon efficient procurement operations.

(f) An efficient procurement operation balances the operations of lean season and flush seasons.

**2. *Methods of Milk Procurement***

A dairy cooperative has to select the potential area for milk production taking into consideration of land utilization pattern, animal husbandry activities, marketable surplus of milk, availability of infrastructural and transport facilities.

A collection center or unit is set up to procure raw milk from a village. Under ideal conditions, the milk potential area for a dairy cooperative can be a radius of 60 to 65 km. The distance to be covered is to be estimated according to climatic conditions, timing of milk collection, and mode of transport. It is essential to see that raw milk reaches the dairy plant at least by 10 a.m., before the atmospheric temperature goes high, especially in the summer seasons, failing which milk turns sour.

While collecting the milk, the milk collector must examine the colour and smell the milk before taking the sample. Sample should be collected from each producer in order to verify the quality of milk in terms of fat content and to check the possibility of adulteration. Milk of poor quality should be rejected and the producer must be warned.

### 3. *Milk Collection Centers*

Milk collection centers organized by dairy cooperatives in important places of its area of operation has the following advantages:

(*a*) They reduce the distance over which the producer must transport his milk.

(*b*) They provide channels of communication between the producer, plant officials, and the cooperatives.

(*c*) They permit convenient distribution of farm inputs such as feeds and fertilizer to the producer.

(*d*) They make it convenient for milk to be tested for quality and advice the producers on clean and good quality of milk.

(*e*) They assure farmers of a market at a reasonable price and thus, give incentive for higher production.

(*f*) They help in pooling small quantities of milk from number of farmers into large amount for easy to transport.

(*g*) They provide necessary cooling facilities for milk and extend the life of milk.

### 4. *Transport Management*

Transport is the basic function to be undertaken by a dairy cooperative. The need to have sound transport system by dairy cooperatives arises due to the following reasons:

(*a*) Milk is a perishable commodity and its life is shorter than vegetables. So, effective use of this material by customers depends on the speedy transport system.

(*b*) The distance between the producer and the consumer is wider and the time available for the distribution of milk is short. Only an efficient transport system will ensure smooth supply of milk.

(c) As milk has short life, its life is extended by chilling the milk. Routing milk supply through chilling plants needs efficient transport system.

(d) Dairy shortages or surpluses can be managed by well organized transport system.

(e) It ensures regular supply of milk to consumers and stabilizes the price of milk in the open market.

5. ***Management of Seasonal Fluctuations***

Milk production in general has two seasons, viz., lean season and flush season. During winter season milk production would be higher. The dairy cooperatives have to balance the demand and supply position. During flush seasons, the surplus milk can be converted into condensed milk powder and byproducts. During lean season, such milk powder can be reconverted as milk and supplied to the consumers. A precondition for the management of seasonal fluctuation is the management of chilling plants and byproduct plants. A well organized transport system also plays the role here. These plants must be operated to their full capacity to avert loss. Maintenance of plants must also be given importance in the capacity utilization. The district level milk cooperatives and regional level federations can play a major role in solving these problems.

**Problems of Dairy Cooperatives**

1. *Seasonal variations:* As milk is not having balanced demand-supply conditions, seasonal variations in production affect the demand-supply position and price level.
2. *Marketing problems:* Milk being a bulky item must be marketed with speed. Otherwise, it may get spoiled and the producer cannot get good price.
3. *Purity of milk:* Milk supplied to the cooperatives must be pure, clean, fresh, and disease-free. Otherwise, a small amount of milk can spoil the entire container.

4. *Disease control:* Milk animals are very often affected by diseases. If enough attention is not taken it may lead to many problems. So, permanent disease control arrangement must be arranged.
5. *Efficient transport system:* Many dairy cooperatives suffer from efficient transport system. Only efficient transport system can make the cooperative success.
6. *Byproducts:* To provide higher price for the producers, dairy cooperatives must engage in the byproduct manufacturing. For this purpose, the regional and national dairy federations must take initiative.
7. *Export avenues:* Dairy products in developing countries have good export avenues and this opportunity must be exploited by the dairy cooperatives.

**Summary**

- Dairy cooperatives have their origin in Europe and they have been organized in developing countries also.
- Dairy as an occupation gives regular income to the farmers.
- Dairy cooperatives have become a boom to the milk producers and they have increased the income and bargaining power of the milk producers.
- In developing countries, there is growing demand for milk, and dairy cooperatives can make the dairy operations successful.
- One of the important activities to be undertaken by the dairy cooperatives is the procurement of milk. Quickness is very important in procuring the milk and dairy cooperatives open milk collection centers in their area of operation.
- An efficient transport system is a precondition for the success of diary cooperatives.
- Dairy cooperatives have specialized the art of managing seasonal fluctuations. During the times of surplus season, surplus milk is converted into milk powder and other

dairy products. During lean season, the milk powder is reconverted into milk and the supply is managed.

- Dairy cooperatives are facing certain problems of seasonal variations, heavy investment for processing units, transport difficulties, and competition in export market.

**Self-learning Activity**

Try to answer the following questions on your own:

1. What are the specific features of dairy industry?
2. Write about milk collection centres.
3. How do dairy cooperatives manage seasonal variations?

# 6 Dairy Cooperatives in India

**Introduction**

Agriculture plays an important role in the Indian economy. About 30 per cent of the national income is derived from agriculture and allied activities like dairying provide livelihood to 64 per cent of the population. Dairy farming plays a key role in providing allied income and employment for millions of people. Because 45 per cent of the households with less than 2 hectares own milch animals, comprising 60 per cent of the milch animals.

The revolution in dairy farming started in the State of Gujarat, located in western part of India. The state though advanced in industries, agriculture development was very poor in the early days. Dairy farming through cooperatives came to help of the farmers. The milk revolution with the dairy cooperatives started their experiments in a place called Anand in Kaira district of Gujarat state in 1946. The success of the dairy cooperatives led to the name "Anand pattern of dairy cooperatives". The special features of Anand pattern of dairy cooperatives are as follows:

1. Organization of dairy cooperatives in every village.
2. All the dairy cooperatives were federated to dairy cooperative union at district level.
3. The dairy cooperative unions looked after the transport arrangements and processing of milk.

4. The farmers were provided weakly payment for their milk.
5. Quality of milk was insisted, which led to quality of dairy products.
6. Farmers were provided with animal husbandry facilities, thereby controlling the cattle disease and preventing the cattle death.
7. Surplus milk was converted into milk byproducts, thereby maintaining an even price of milk and milk products throughout the year.

**Operation Flood**

Operation Flood was the strategy adopted by the government of India through which the Anand pattern of dairy cooperatives was popularized. Operation Flood was designed to create a 'flood' of milk by helping rural producers to organize village diary cooperatives on the pattern of Anand, thereby gaining access to and control over a network of milk processing facilities and finally the urban market. During the year 1965, the National Dairy Development Board was established under the Ministry of Agriculture with the task of organizing milk producers' cooperatives throughout the country. This led to the introduction of the Operation Flood scheme to replicate Anand pattern of dairy development. In 1970 the *first phase of Operation Flood* was introduced (1970-1981). The purpose of Operation Flood-I was to link the four metro cities with 18 potential milksheds, which was later, extended to 27 milksheds. Operation Flood-II was introduced between 1979-1985 and Operation Flood-III was between 1985-1990. Through this Operation Flood schemes, milk production expanded with processing, marketing, productivity, institutional viability and professional management.

**Salient Features of Operation Flood**

1. Promoting village dairy cooperatives and cooperative unions.

2. Creation of additional milk chilling, processing, distribution, and marketing facilities to be owned and operated by Dairy Cooperative Unions.
3. Creation of sufficient conversion capacities with the cooperative dairies for balancing the lean and flush supplies.
4. Establishment of a network of storage and long distance milk transport facilities to enable the operation of a national milk grid.
5. Equipping the dairy cooperatives with milk production enhancement inputs to improve productivity of milk animals.
6. Development and provision of support services such as information systems, training and manpower services for the cooperatives.
7. Establishment and management of centralized support services such as animal disease diagnostic centers, vaccine and biological production and delivery systems and a national frozen semen system to enhance the productivity of dairy animals.
8. Promotion and development of indigenous dairy processing and conservation methods and the establishment of dairy machinery and equipment manufacturing facilities in the country in order to cater to the need of a growing dairy industry.
9. Establishment facilities and undertaking research and development activities.
10. Development of three tier dairy cooperatives starting from village level, district level, and state level.
11. A National Dairy Development Board (1965) made responsible for project planning and technical advice and the Indian Dairy Corporation (1970) responsible for financing these cooperatives.

## Strategies adopted for Operation Flood

The Operation Flood scheme followed three important strategies namely, strategic, institutional, and technological approaches.

### Strategic Approach

Through this strategic approach, food aid got from foreign countries has been invested towards the development of dairy industry. One of the major focuses was market. The food aid helped to expand urban milk supply schemes and the funds generated were ploughed back between producers and consumers. The concept of *Mother Dairy* was developed, which is a city dairy that would provide the milk producers a good price and establish a linkage between the centers of production and consumption.

Another strategic approach was managing the seasonality through crop dairy complementary activities. The food aid was serving as a buffer stock to balance the seasonality in milk production. In surplus season, milk products were made and a good price was guaranteed to the farmers.

The next strategy was the indigenisation of the dairy industry; by promoting local industries and making the country self-sufficient in producing machineries for milk industry and allied industries.

### Institutional Approach

The institutional approach of Operation Flood led to the promotion of grass-root level democracy of cooperatives. The village cooperatives, the district milk cooperative unions and the state federations formed the basis of institutional development. Cooperative democracy was introduced at all levels. To help the dairy cooperatives, professional management and training establishments were organized. To help these cooperatives, a National Cooperative Dairy Federation of India (NCDFI) was established at the national level. The purpose of this national federation is to establish National Milk Grid (NMG) and link the deficit areas with surplus areas.

### Technological Approach

The technological approach of Operation Flood emphasizes on proper marketing system, an incentive-led development strategy for achieving productivity and improved farm income. For this purpose, new technology has been introduced to give price incentive to the farmers by insisting them to purchase needed inputs and to get technical knowledge. Technology was also introduced in productivity, efficiency and in the socio-economic well-being of farmers. Technology played an important role in milk collection by proper testing for fairness in payment, in transportation, quality and value addition, and in marketing for hygienic and timely distribution. Inputs in the form of feed supplements, health care facilities, genetic improvement of milch animals, immunization, effective utilization of crop residues, etc. were introduced through cooperatives.

### Impact of Operation Flood Schemes

India has introduced three phases of operation flood schemes. Milk production, which was 23 million tones per annum during 1970s rose to the level of 69 million tones per annum in 1996/97 making India the second largest milk producer in world. By this time there were about 74,500 village dairy cooperatives federated to 170 district milk unions across the country. Around 10 million farmers have become members of the dairy cooperatives. During 1997/98 dairy cooperatives collected on an average 12.26 million liters of milk every day. Commercial imports of dairy products were stopped completely from 1975. The four major cities, namely, Delhi, Bombay, Calcutta, and Madras accounted for 40 per cent of milk marketed by the cooperatives and Operation Flood dairies. All together Operation Flood dairies in metropolitan areas marketed around 3.2 million liters of milk per day. Other cities and towns accounted for a sale of 4.8 million liters of milk by cooperative daily. During the year 2002 India became the largest producer of milk in the world. This was possible due to diary cooperatives.

## Economic and Social Impact of Dairy Cooperatives

1. Through dairy cooperatives, the income of the farmers increased by lowering the cost and increasing the efficiency of milk production.
2. The cooperatives provided needed services to the farmers and faced the competition from the private traders.
3. The cooperatives have trained large number of villagers to a level of skilled workers and increased their efficiency.
4. Dairy as an occupation was made a reliable one through regular payments to meet the household expenditures and making crop income to finance investments on agriculture.
5. The cooperatives have provided poverty-oriented programmes, such as credit and facilities to purchase dairy animals, biogas construction, and improved water facility.
6. For the landless labourers, cooperative dairying has become a reliable occupation.
7. Operation Flood in collaboration with NGOs, has established more than 6,000 women dairy cooperatives and empowered the women.
8. High income elasticity of demand for education was made in Indian villages through dairy cooperatives and Operation Flood.
9. The dairy cooperatives in India combated poverty by providing productive employment and milk marketing through dairy cooperatives effected nutrition, income, job creation, education, and empowerment of women, particularly among smallholder dairy farms.

## Organizational Structure of Dairy Cooperatives in India

The foundation of Anand Pattern of milk cooperatives was laid with the organization of the Kaira Dist. Coop. Milk Producers' Union Limited at Anand. In this pattern all the functions of dairying—milk production, procurement, processing and marketing—are controlled by the milk producers themselves. In addition to this, all the facilities related to milk production and procurement are provided at farmers' doorsteps.

The basic unit in the Anand Pattern is the Village Milk Producers' Co-operative—a voluntary association of milk producers in a village, who wish to market their milk collectively. All the Village Milk Producers' Cooperatives in a district are members of their District Co-operative Milk Producers' Union.

Every milk producer can become a member of the co-operative society. At a general meeting of members, representatives are elected to form a managing committee, which manages the day-to-day affairs of milk. Collection, and its testing for fat content, sale of cattle feed etc. Each society also provides Artificial Insemination (AI) services and veterinary first-aid. Each milk producer's milk is tested and paid for on the basis of the quality of milk. Usually the morning milk is paid for in the evening and the evening milk is paid for in the next morning. The village societies also market nutritionally balanced compounded cattle feed produced by cattle feed plant owned and operated by the district-level union. The balanced cattle feed is sold on a no-profit-no-loss basis.

The primary milk producers' societies are affiliated to a district union, which owns and operates a feeder/balancing dairy; cattle feed plant and facilities for production of semen and its distribution. The Union also operates a network of veterinarians to provide routine and emergency services for animal health care. The village's societies elect the Board of Directors of the Union, which is responsible for the day-to-day management of the Union's centralized facilities for milk collection, processing and marketing of inputs. A Managing Director, who reports to the elected Chairman and the Board of Directors, professionally manages each Union.

The dairy, owned by a Union, usually has a milk drying plant to convert the seasonal surpluses into milk powder and other conserved products. With the help of the drying plant, the Union is able to ensure that the milk producers get 80-90 per cent of the lean season price even in the flush season. The farmers are, therefore, able to get a good price for the bulk of the milk, which is produced in the flush season. This has enabled the farmers to get 20-40 per cent higher prices than what they would have got if they were not parts of the co-operative system. The middlemen have usually been paying only 50-60 per cent of the lean season price in the flush season.

Bulk of the out-of-pocket expenditure on milk production is the purchase of cattle feed concentrates like oil cakes, cottonseeds etc. The cattle feed plant owned and operated by the co-operative is able to provide nutritionally balanced cattle feed at prices 20-30 per cent lower than the prices of the traditional feeds. The milk producers are therefore able to substantially increase their returns from milk production because of the better returns for their milk and lower feeding costs. The milk collected from the villages is usually sent to the co-operative dairy through trucks hired by the co-operatives. Each co-operative dairy tries to market the bulk of its milk as liquid milk and converts the surplus milk into products. Professional managers employed by the co-operative ensure that they get the best returns for their produce. The profits made by the dairy are redistributed to the milk producers as a subsidiary payment. Many societies are able to pay 12-15 per cent bonus to their milk producers based on the business contributed to the co-operative.

**Management**

A Managing Committee of nine members is elected democratically by the members of society in a general meeting. From amongst the members one-third of these committee members retire every year and are replaced in an election by secret ballot. The Chairperson of the committee retires every year as well. The Managing Committee sets the cooperative's policies and selects the society staff including a secretary, a milk collector, a fat tester, a clerk: an inseminator, an Accountant and a Helper to perform the society's work/ administration, depending upon the size of business.

To start with, a union supervisor helps the new society to organize its day-to-day business and to become economically viable in about three months period. It is then recommended by the union for registration to the State Cooperative Department. Every society is constantly guided, supervised and controlled by the Union, to keep them strong and viable. There is a continuous and concurrent audit of all the societies on a quarterly basis to ensure a clean milk business. Apart from this, there is an annual statutory audit.

**Functions**

Every morning and evening, the society buys the surplus milk from the member-producers and non-members. The producer is paid for the milk usually within twelve hours (mostly when the producer returns to the society to sell more milk next time). The payment is made on the basis of fat content of milk supplied by individual producer. The union's dairy plant organizes the transport of milk twice daily from all its member-societies.

The producers in this system are not only assured of regular and remunerative payment for their milk but also benefit from the milk production enhancement inputs. The micro-level inputs such as veterinary first aid and artificial insemination are organized by village societies. One staff member of the society is trained for carrying out these functions. In addition, the supply of balanced cattle feed and the sale of fodder seeds are also channelized through the societies.

**Distribution of Profits**

The net profit earned by the society is distributed to the members as per the provisions of Act. Out of the net profit earned by the society in a year, 25 per cent is contributed to its reserve fund, not exceeding 12 per cent is paid as dividend to the share-holders on the paid-up share capital, and small contributions depending upon provision in State Cooperative Act are made to education fund. Out of the balance, 65 per cent is paid as bonus to the members in proportion to their milk sales to the society, 10 per cent is contributed to cattle development fund, 10 per cent is contributed to charity, 5 per cent to co-operative propaganda, and balance 10 per cent to staff bonus.

**District Dairy Cooperative Union**

A key element in the Anand Pattern of Dairy Cooperative is that all registered village milk societies are members of a district cooperative milk producers' union, which enable them jointly to own a dairy processing factory and a cattle feed plant. In order to become member of the union, a registered society must purchase at least one share of Rs. 100 and pay Rs. 5 as entrance fee (Birr 1 = Rs. 3)

**Management**

A Board of Directors, consisting of sixteen to seventeen members, of which twelve controls the Union, are democratically elected from amongst the representatives of the village societies. The remaining five comprise the Managing Director as a member-secretary, one or two representatives of the financing institution, a representative of the Registrar Cooperative Societies, and a representative of the Federation. These five members are not eligible for contesting to the post of Chairman. The Chairman is elected by the members of the Board of Directors by secret ballot. One-third of the elected Board members retire every year by rotation so that each member functions for three years. This also ensures continuity of management.

The general policy for the union is framed by the Board in which is also vested all the powers regarding management of the organization. The Board employs the Managing Director/General Manager. His removal, however, has to be done by the general body (representing chairman of all the affiliated societies) with the prior approval of IDC. While the Board determines the number, type and scales of posts, it is the Managing Director/General Manager who makes the appointment of junior staff. A sound code of conduct and administrative discipline is maintained between Board of Directors and the administrators of the Union.

### Functions

In general, the Union carries out five important functions: procurement, processing and marketing of milk. Providing technical inputs, strengthening of milk cooperative movement, organization of extension activities and rural development services. The Union owns and operates dairy plant; cattle feed plant, fodder and bull mother farms, semen collection station, headquarter center for animal husbandry activities.

In addition to above, the Union carries out research development and other promotional activities for the overall benefit of farmers. The Union organizes the macro-level inputs such as compounded cattle feed, fodder seeds, and various veterinary services including round the clock emergency visits of veterinary doctors for treatment of sick animals, all of which are supplied to the milk producers at their door-steps, through their own milk cooperative societies. The total cost of these programmes is included in the milk price structure and amounts to about 6-8 paise per kg of milk procured. Thus, it is at the Union level that professional skills are hired for specialized purposes, which individual producers cannot afford to do. The union pays to the producer's dividends on their shares and bonus in relation to the quantity of milk supplied by them during the year. The milk products processed by the union are marketed through the Federation.

A special feature of the Anand Pattern is that the unions are under continuous and concurrent audit to maintain financial propriety.

### Distribution of Profits

On the net profit earned by the union, 25 per cent is carried to its reserve fund, small contribution is made to education fund as required by the State Cooperative Act and a sum not exceeding 12 per cent per annum is paid to member societies as dividend on their paid-up share capital. Out of the remaining profits the distribution is done as per Cooperative Societies Act in the following manner. Upto 80 per cent as bonus to the members in proportion to milk supplies; 10 per cent towards charity fund, 5 per cent towards cooperative propaganda fund; 3 per cent towards research in the dairy industry and 2 per cent towards dividend equalization fund.

**Cooperative Milk Marketing Federation**

The District Dairy Cooperative Unions become members of a Cooperative Milk Marketing Federation by subscribing to it at least Rs. 20,000 each as share capital. The Federation is responsible for evolving and implementation of policies on cooperative marketing of all member unions' liquid milk and milk products, deciding the product-price mix, cooperative provision of joint services (artificial insemination, breeding, etc.) and cooperative marketing of technical inputs to members.

**Management**

The Federation's Board consists mainly of the elected Chairmen of all the member unions and the Federation's Managing Director. Other members are the representative of Registrar, Cooperative Societies; a representative of financing agency nominee of NDDB and one nominee of the State Government (Dairy Development Department). Each member has voting right. The members elect a Chairman of the Board. The Board evolves the Federation's policies on all its functions. Members' votes are weighed by the amount of milk procured by each union in the previous year and any profit distribution is done on the same basis.

The Federation's Board is advised by its Management Committee, which is composed of each member union's chief executive, the Federation's Chief Quality Control Officer and one or more non-voting co-opted technical representatives of NDDB. The Federation's Managing Director is the Committee's Chairman, and the General Manager it's Secretary. The Management Committee meets once monthly and is also responsible for day-to-day implementation of the Board's policies and plans.

**Distribution of Profits**

Of the total profit earned by the federation 25 per cent goes to its reserve fund. The member unions are paid dividend not exceeding 12 per cent on the paid-up share capital. After making small contributions to education and other funds as required by the Cooperative Act, the balance is distributed as bonus to member unions and/or shall be taken to general fund and/or will be utilized for research and development as decided by the General Meeting.

**Summary**

- India is the largest producer of milk since 2002. This was possible due to the efforts of dairy cooperatives.
- Dairy cooperatives in India have been organized on the model Anand Pattern. Anand Pattern of dairy cooperatives are organized in every village. They organize diary cooperative unions to look after transport and procurement of milk. Farmers are paid every week by the cooperative.
- Operation Flood was introduced in India in the year 1970. Three Operation Floods have been completed, which led to the increase in milk production.
- Out of Operation Flood and the organization of dairy cooperative on Anand Pattern, have increased the standard of living of the farmers. Dairy as an important allied occupation has been providing regular income to the farmers. One of the beneficiaries of dairy cooperatives is the women folk.

- The organizational structure of primary dairy cooperatives is based on Anand Pattern, which specifies one dairy cooperative for one village and federating such dairy cooperatives with a district dairy cooperative union.
- The district dairy cooperative unions arrange transport facilities and milk processing units. The district unions help the primary cooperatives in providing value addition to the products.

**Self-learning Activity**

Try to answer the following questions on your own.

1. Give an account of Strategic Approach of Operation Flood.
2. What are the features of ANAND Pattern of dairy cooperatives?
3. What lessons can be learned from the success of Indian dairy cooperatives?

# 7 Dairy Cooperative Movement in Denmark and Ethiopia

## Dairy Cooperatives in Denmark

### *Background*

Denmark is the homeland of agricultural cooperation in the world. One of the most interesting and essential features of the Danish cooperative moment is its voluntary development. It is a voluntary movement by the producers and consumers who wanted, and were able, by their own efforts to tackle their economic problem wholly or partly in collaboration with their fellow countrymen. Besides this feature, we find that to an exceptional degree the movement is self-made, introduced and nourished by common men who make up the membership of the cooperative societies, without any advice or support from abroad, without State control or State help. Denmark has no cooperative legislation. The different types of cooperative activities have been organized freely, adjusting themselves according to local needs and conditions. Owing to the absence of cooperative legislation the cooperative movement presents varying forms ranging from strict conformity to the classical Rochadale stores to semi-public institutions. The basic principle guiding the movement has been to strive on a no-profit basis for the direct economic benefit of the members who have founded the societies and are their sole owners. The voluntary cooperative movement organized on democratic lines has been serving the Danish families in the villages and in towns since the last quarter of the last century and will continue to serve for ages. The Danish movement is a superb example of voluntary effort of common men for alleviating their economic, political and social status. In this respect Denmark is the torch bearer to other countries of the world.

Surprisingly, the cooperative movement in Denmark was started with the establishment of consumers' stores in accordance with the Rochadale principles. The first cooperative store was established in 1886 in Thisted. In 1882, the growth of the movement was started in Hjedding, a village in Jutland. The growth of the movement was quite rapid in rural areas. The members of this cooperative dairy agreed among themselves that they would deliver all their surplus milk to it, and distribute profits in proportion to the quantity of the milk supplied. Liability was to be a joint responsibility of the members. In the following years a large number of cooperative dairies were started. The bacon factory was started in 1887 and marketing associations of eggs came into being in 1895. Subsequently, associations for the export of butter, for the sale of fruits and vegetables, for the purchase of artificial manures and feeding stuff, etc., were also started. Since the history of the cooperative movement in Denmark is the history of the growth and development of agricultural cooperation, we shall, after making a passing reference to the consumers' movement, concentrate our attention on the agricultural cooperative movement and discuss it at length.

**Cooperative Dairies**

The first agricultural society, viz., the Royal Agricultural Society was organized in 1769 with the chief objective of developing agriculture. By and by, the number of such societies increased. These societies improved the condition of the farmers. During the last century the Danish farmers were mainly dependent upon the production and export of grain. They had to change to dairy farming mainly because they could not compete with America and European countries in the supply of cheap corn and also because of an increase in the demand for Danish butter in England. In the beginning, butter was produced by ordinary churning method. It was in 1880 that the use of cream separating machine was made and number of private creameries came into being. In 1882, a cooperative creamery was set up in Hjedding. This creamery proved to be a great success. Encouraged by it, many other cooperative creameries were set up in the country. And today, the cooperative dairies occupy the front position in the cooperative system of Denmark. The area of operation being small, fresh supplies of milk can be had every day. There are no transport bottle necks and no storage difficulties are faced. After the butter and cream have been taken out, the skimmed milk is given to the farmers which is used as a cattle feed. The butter making process in Denmark is a highly specialized one. The cooperative dairies employ highly technically skilled staff.

**Special Features**

The cooperative dairies of Denmark have the following special features:

1. The product is immediately connected with the raising of raw materials.
2. The manufacturing is done on the land close to the place of production. Consequently, there is saving of time. The cost of production is minimum since no transportation cost is involved.
3. The primary cooperative societies deal with the various problems of industrial organization.
4. On account of specialization, highest standards of efficiency are maintained, and the price of the produce is quite low.
5. The marketing system is highly organized. Consequently, all the economies of large-scale buying and production are enjoyed by the farmers. They employ trained staff who possess day-to-day knowledge of market requirements, and, therefore, they are able to cut down

the cost to the minimum. Their method of packing is excellent, specially suited to trans-shipment for export.

**Advantages of Marketing by Federations**

In Denmark the entire export trade is controlled by federations. Marketing through federations has a number of advantages:

1. Because of the transportation of goods in bulk, cheaper transport facilities can be availed of.
2. Secondly, the dairy products have been standardized in quality, packing, finishing, etc.
3. Thirdly, the cost of packing is very low.
4. Fourthly, there are no middlemen or selling agents.
5. Finally, the process is stabilized and competition is avoided.

The local societies are supplied with up-to-date information. The Danish Cooperative dairies are not only interested in business but are also interested in improving the economic condition of the farmers. It has been fully realized by them that the interests of the trader and the producer can come together. They try to get the farmers high price for their products. They impart training to the farmer not only in business methods but also in cattle rearing. The farmer is made to realize that his interest is linked with the reputation of the Danish dairies. The education in the principles and methods of production is therefore, automatic and is imparted through practice.

A few details about the working of cooperative dairies, distribution of profits, raising of funds, etc., are worth mentioning here.

**Constitution and Working**

Members are required to supply milk according to the terms of contract, which continues for 15 to 20 years after which the dairy is wound up and started afresh. The farmers take loan from the commercial bank or a savings bank for the purchase of machinery and equipment. The milk is collected from the members daily. It is tested and pasteurized. The cream is separated from the milk and butter is prepared. Skimmed milk is given back to the farmers for being used as cattle feed. The farmers are paid according to the fat contents of the milk supplied by them. In case the contents in the milk are less than 28 per cent, the farmers are instructed to improve the quality. The improper feeding and adulteration of milk are punished with heavy fines and persistent defaulters are dismissed from the membership of the dairy. The chief functions performed by the dairy cooperatives are:

1. To process the milk supplied by the members;
2. To provide funds for investment; and
3. To give advice on cattle keeping and to provide technical knowledge regarding feeding and breeding of the animals.

The cooperative dairies have set up their creameries in central places in their area of operation. The goods produced by these dairies are sold under the trademark "LURBRAND". It is a mark of quality and goods bearing this seal are easily sold out in Denmark, England and Germany. The principles followed by these dairies are:

1. Open membership within the area of operation;
2. Democratic management; and
3. Distribution of profits in proportion to the value of milk supplied by the members.

***Capital***

The working capital of the dairy is raised from the members. The members are paid interest on these deposits. The rate of interest is quite low. The initial capital of the cooperative is raised from a bank and is repaid out of the profits.

***Profits***

In the beginning a fixed rate of profit is allowed on the capital and afterwards it is deposited into the reserve fund and whatever is left, is distributed among the members in proportion to the value of the milk supplied.

In 1976 there were 217 dairy cooperatives and associations totalling 311 installations. Among these, 53 receive more than 15 million kg. a year whole the smallest 136 dairies, with less than 10 million kg. together received 16 per cent of the milk.

**Circumstances that Led to the Organization of Dairy Cooperatives in Denmark**

The circumstances that led to the organization of dairy cooperatives and the performance of dairy cooperatives in Denmark were as follows:

1. Denmark being a small country was not having good soil for the production of wheat. Due to necessity they cultivated wheat. But they could not compete with other big European countries in producing wheat. So, the Danish farmers were in a position to diversify their farming for survival.
2. Instead of selling wheat, the farmers found that wheat can be used as feed for cows and milk & milk products can be produced. This idea led to the organization of dairy cooperatives.
3. The farmers in Denmark were smallholders and there was a necessity for them to consolidate their efforts through cooperative dairying.
4. Cooperative dairying provided value addition to milk products and they had very good demand in export market. This paved the way for a higher income to the farmers.
5. The Folk schools of Denmark organized by the Cooperator Grundtvig gave needed training to the young farmers in the field of dairying and organizing dairy cooperatives.
6. One of the reasons for their success was the organization of federal type of dairy cooperative starting from village level to national level.

7. The quality of the products was very high and the Danish dairy cooperatives used the trade name "LUR BRAND" for their products.
8. The country started manufacturing dairy industry machineries that led to the revolution of dairy activities.
9. All the farmers were educated, which helped to run their cooperatives successfully.
10. The combined effort through cooperatives kept the private dairy sector away from competition.

**Factors Responsible for the Success of the Cooperative Dairies**

The success achieved by the cooperative dairies in Denmark can be attributed to the following factors:

1. The manufacturing of products close to the place of production has been responsible for keeping the cost of production minimum.
2. The principle of unlimited liability has made the member to take keen interest in the working of the dairy.
3. Owing to the policy of prompt payments made to the members for the milk supplied by the members' loyalty is assured.
4. The policy of making payment for the milk according to its fat contents ensures the supply of good quality milk.
5. The importance attached to proper feeding of the cattle and the system of testing the dairy cattle, and the breeding of the cattle by the control societies and cattle breeding societies respectively has not only led to the improvement of the breed of the cattle but has also led to the improvement of the quality of the milk.
6. The services offered by the butter export associations to the local dairies have not brought profits to the members only but to the society as well.
7. Production and export of butter under the trade mark 'LURBRAND' has not only led to the standardization of the production of butter but also assured the consumers of supply of good quality butter.

8. The use of highly sophisticated machines and specialized techniques for the production of butter has established the reputation of the Danish Cooperative Dairies on a firm footing.

**Dairy Cooperatives in Ethiopia**

Ethiopia is an agricultural country and has the largest cattle population in Africa, comprising 26 million cattle, 24 million sheep, 17 million goats, 7 million equines, 1 million camels, and 52 million poultry (FAO, 1981). In 1984 there were about 8.33 million cows and heifers older than two years, of which 65 per cent were yielding milk. Milk production in Ethiopia grew by 1.7 per cent between 1965 and 1976 and by 1.1 per cent per year from 1976 to 1985. During 1981 milk produced in Ethiopia was 27 kg per person. It dropped to 17 kg/person during 1985. But it is still higher than the Sub-Saharan African average of 15.7 kg/person. By 1983 local cows produced 400 to 680 kg of milk per lactation period of less than 7 months.

**Milk Production**

Sour milk or yoghurt is produced in the traditional system by leaving the fresh milk to sour for few days. Soured milk keeps longer than raw milk, so this process is useful for storing milk during the days of Wednesday and Friday where Coptic Christians are forbidden to consume animal products. Sour milk, not consumed at home, is usually sold to neighbours.

Sour milk can also be churned to make butter. The byproduct buttermilk is rarely sold and it is fed to calves, consumed at home, or further processed. Ethiopian farmers prefer butter manufacturing and indigenous methods are followed.

**Production Systems**

Milk production system in Ethiopia is followed on the following pattern:

1. ***Pastoralism:*** Pastoralists are livestock owners who maintain natural grasslands in arid areas (lowlands) with their herds of camel, sheep, goat, and cattle. Pastoralists

move from one place to another place searching for fresh grazing areas. Milk is the main source of food for pastoralists.

2. *Agro pastoralists:* They are the farmers who cultivate food crops for food and for sale. Their livestock are fed on grazing land and crop land after harvest. Livestock are used for draught, milk production, and savings.
3. *Mixed Farming:* Food or cash crop cultivation is the main activity. The farm size will be very small ranging from one to five hectares. Livestock are kept for draught, milk, and meat.
4. *Intensive Dairy Farming:* These farmers do dairy farming intensively and cultivate fodder crops exclusively. The dairy animals are not used for draught but manure is used for growing fodder. Milk is a major source of farm income. Labour intensity is high in this system.
5. *Peri-urban Milk Production:* This system is developed around cities that have high demand for milk. Milk is traded directly to the consumers of the city and is the major source of income to the farmers.

**Measures to Improve Milk Production in Ethiopia**

1. *Reduced mortality of stock:* Efforts must be taken to protect cattle against the major diseases such as East Coast fever and tick-borne diseases.
2. *Lower calving intervals:* These are necessary to increase the number of calves born and to reduce the period when cows are not producing milk.
3. *Improved calve rearing:* This is necessary to ensure that a greater proportion of pure bred and cross bred are born and reared to reduce mortality.
4. *Upgrading indigenous stock:* In the short run it will be beneficial to the farmers to improve the productivity of indigenous stock through cross-breeding and better management.
5. *Adequate levels of feeding:* Efforts should be taken to reduce dry season shortage of feed. Such crops as maize, sorghum, and elephant grass must be used as feeding stuff.

6. ***Commercial dairying:*** Commercial dairying through cooperatives with production and market orientation must be encouraged to make the dairy farming a successful venture.

## Dairy Cooperatives in Ethiopia

There are two types of dairy cooperatives organized in Ethiopia. One by the producer cooperatives and the other by the service cooperatives. There are about 98 producer and service dairy cooperatives in Ethiopia. Exclusive dairy cooperatives were not organized in Ethiopia. Dairy Development Enterprise (DDE), a government enterprise, was having 14 dairy state farms under its control. These dairy farms supplied milk to Addis Ababa city.

## Scope for Organizing Dairy Cooperatives in Ethiopia

The scope for organizing dairy cooperatives in Ethiopia is very high. The following factors favor the speedy organization of dairy cooperatives in Ethiopia:

1. The high cattle population and dairy animals favor an atmosphere for increased production of milk and milk products through dairy cooperatives.
2. The farmers are traditionally experienced in managing dairy farming and they can improve their conditions by organizing dairy cooperatives.
3. With the economy moving fast, the income of the population is increasing, which may result in higher consumption of milk.
4. Milk being an essential food for children, the scope is very high to increase milk production through dairy cooperatives.
5. Enormous scope is there to have an export market. By means of setting processing units by dairy cooperatives, milk products can be exported to other countries.
6. The atmosphere with the government is favorable for the organization of dairy cooperatives in Ethiopia.

7. International help through NGOs can be available to organize diary cooperatives and dairy industries.

**Summary**

- Denmark is the pioneering country in the organization of dairy cooperatives and the Danish economy and export to a great extent depend on dairy cooperatives.
- Dairy cooperatives in Denmark were organized under circumstances, like competition from European countries in wheat production, hardships of the farmers, and the example of Rochdale Pioneers.
- Dairy cooperatives in Denmark are not only exporting dairy products, but also provide solid income to the farmers, engage in byproduct activities, and manufacture diary instruments.
- Ethiopia is the largest country in Africa having sizeable livestock population. Dairy development is not new to the farmers. Various types of dairy development like pastoralism, agro-pastoralism, mixed farming, etc have their own stake in dairy development.
- Ethiopia has enormous scope to increase milk production through organization of dairy cooperatives. It can take the example of the neighboring country, Kenya, in producing and exporting dairy products through dairy cooperatives.

**Self-learning Activity**

Try to answer the following questions on your own:

1. What are the special features of Danish dairy cooperatives?
2. Explain the milk production system in Ethiopia.
3. What is existing position of dairy cooperatives in Ethiopia?

# 8 Forest Cooperatives

**Importance of Forest**

1. In any geographical area, forest area forms a major part and they are very vital for the economic and agriculture development of a country. In countries where natural forests are not there, artificial forests are created using modern agricultural technology.
2. The rainfall of a country is contributed by the size of forest and thickness of forest. In whichever country forests are reduced, the rainfall has also come down in such countries.
3. A well-grown forest is necessary for the development of flora and fauna. Forests are the abode of numerous plants and trees. They are also the home for species, birds and living beings.
4. The sustainability of wild animals like lion, tiger, elephant, etc., depends on the size of forest. Because such wild animals need enormous moving space, plants, water, and protection, which are available only in forests.
5. Forest area provide livelihood to tribal population, who form major part of population in several countries. Such tribal populations make their living in mountains, which are covered by thick forests.
6. Forest provides construction materials like wood. In many countries, organized felling of trees is not taking place.

Indiscriminate cutting of trees is depleting the forest area. In several African and South American countries, illegal cutting of trees is creating a major problem.

7. Many of the rare medicinal plants are available in forest areas. Such rare medicinal plants can grow well only in forest areas, where they get huge rain and fertile soil.
8. Minor forest produces like honey, beedi leaf, charcoal, etc., give employment opportunity and marketing scope for many people. These materials are collected by the tribal population.
9. Well-grown forest through afforestation controls soil erosion. Soil erosion is a great problem in African countries and to Ethiopia also. By means of the soil erosion, the topsoil is removed and the fertility of the soil is getting reduced.
10. Conserving forest is a pre-condition for environmental development and for the control of environmental degradation. In many countries, separate ministries have been created to protect the forests and the environment.

## Forest Cooperatives

Forest cooperatives have been organized in countries where sizeable forest lands are available. Forest cooperatives are employment-oriented and they undertake multi-purpose functioning.

## Objectives of Forest Cooperatives

1. To advice the members on modern methods of forest exploitation and management.
2. Maintaining a common tree nursery to obtain materials for replanting the cleared areas.
3. Drawing up a joint afforestation programme, coordinating the cutting of timber and replanting.
4. Providing pest control schemes for common action in the case of infection and supplying pesticides.

5. Setting up joint fire prevention service by establishing a vigilance team, recruiting guards, and maintaining fire-fighting equipments.
6. Building and maintaining forest roads to facilitate transport.
7. Employing labour force to cut timber and to maintain a common camp for the workers.
8. Transporting timber in special vehicles from the members' forest area to the market.
9. Processing timber in a common saw or pulp-mill or in similar factories.

**Organization and Membership of Forest Cooperatives**

Forest cooperatives are mainly organized among tribal population, whose characteristics are as follows:

1. They are away from the civilized society. So, they may not have proper education and awareness about the maintenance of forests.
2. They consist of tribal population. These are special group of population who make their living only in forest and hill areas.
3. Their level of education is low because to construct schools and educational institutions in remote areas would be a challenge to the community.
4. Their entire livelihood and needs are surrounded by forest. As they are away from the plains, they make their employment and livelihood around the forest. They come to the plains only to purchase certain essential goods like salt, medicine, etc once in few days or months.
5. They collect minor forest produces and market them in the plains. Their life is surrounded by the collection of these produces.
6. They have less access to institutional credit and marketing facilities. Due to lack of awareness of the cooperatives, such institutions are yet to reach them. Government initiative is necessary to organize such institutions.

7. They are being exploited by moneylenders. Like the farmers and fishermen, the tribal populations are also exploited by the moneylender for quite a long time.
8. Their food habits are related to forest and rarely they do agriculture. But nowadays, due to the reduction in the size of forests, they have started learning agriculture also.
9. Their occupation is controlled by Government regulations on forests. In many countries, forestlands belong to the government. So, governments impose strict regulations to use the forest resources.
10. Governmental help reach such people very slowly. Due to their remoteness, government agencies are unable to reach them. Difficulties of transport and communication are also giving a challenge to government help.

## Benefits of Forest Cooperatives to the Members

Forest cooperatives are organized by the tribal population or people who are living in forest areas. Many NGOs have started helping the tribal population by means of initiating the organization of cooperatives for the tribal population. Following are the benefits of forest cooperatives to the members.

1. Cooperatives provide collective effort in all their functioning. People who are living in forest areas are scattered and they live in groups. Cooperatives provide an opportunity to mobilize their efforts for joint development.
2. Exploitation moneylenders has been avoided. Moneylenders, using poverty and financial difficulties of the forest people, provide them money whenever they ask but while collecting the money, they charge high interest rate. In many cases, tribals have become bonded labourers to the moneylenders. Cooperatives are able to change the situation.

3. Better credit and marketing facilities are provided to them. Forest cooperatives undertake multipurpose activities. They provide credit, marketing, processing, consumer, and other related services to the members. Such multi-purpose activities are very convenient to the members.
4. Income guarantee is provided by the cooperatives. By means of marketing the forest produces from the members regularly, the forest cooperatives provide a guaranteed income to the members. Even during seasons where there is non-availability of forest produces, the members are engaged in developing nursery plants, which also give them good income.
5. Welfare facilities like education, transport, communication, etc., are also provided by the cooperatives. Forest cooperatives do not stop with providing credit and other services to the members. As the forest areas are remote, they provide education, transport, and communication facilities to the members.

**Functions of Forest Cooperatives**

Forest cooperatives have the following objectives and discharge the following functions:

1. *Providing extension service and advice:* The members are provided with extension service and advice on modern methods of forest management and exploitation. As the majority of the members of forest cooperatives are illiterate and ignorant of forest wealth, they are to be given proper awareness and education about forest wealth through extension services. Such activities can be undertaken by the forest cooperatives.
2. *Maintaining common tree nurseries:* For further growth of forest, forest cooperatives make it a point to develop the forest nurseries to compensate the loss of trees due to cutting of trees. Such nurseries are developed either in the premises of the forest cooperatives or in the hill areas where good location exists.

3. *Drawing a joint afforestation programme:* Though the forest areas belong to the government, certain times governments allot forestlands to the cooperatives. Cooperatives make it a point for the phased cutting of trees and replanting the trees in the same place.
4. *Providing pest control schemes:* Now-a-days, forest is also affected by pest attack. Forest cooperatives through the government agencies go for aerial spraying of pesticides to control the pest attack on forest trees.
5. *Providing credit and marketing facilities:* This is considered to be one of the major functions of the forest cooperatives. To release the members from the cruelty of moneylenders, cooperatives are providing credit and marketing facilities.
6. *Providing fire prevention measures:* Forests are susceptible to fire very frequently. This happens in areas of thick forest. Forest cooperatives make it a point to give training to the members on fire prevention measures and they keep ready the fire-fighting equipments.
7. *Constructing and maintaining forest roads:* Transport facilities are very much needed for the members of the forest cooperatives to come to the plains and purchase and sell commodities. Though this is an important duty of the government, small roads and link roads are constructed and maintained by forest cooperatives.
8. *To provide employment opportunity to the members:* This is also one of the major objectives of the forest cooperatives. The forest produces that are collected are told to the members. The period of collection is also told to the members. After the produces are collected, they are sold in the market on behalf of the members.
9. *Providing social and welfare amenities* like school, medical facilities, transport, communication facilities, etc. As the tribal population and population in the forest areas find it difficult to get these welfare facilities, forest cooperatives arrange such facilities to the members.

## Working of Forest Cooperatives

### *Membership*

The membership of forest cooperatives is exclusive to the tribal population and the population living in forest areas. Moneylenders and merchants are not allowed to become the members of forest cooperatives.

### Working Capital

The working capital of forest cooperatives consists of owned funds and borrowed funds. Members contribute owned fund, in the form of capital. The members of forest cooperatives are very poor and we cannot expect high contribution from them. So in many countries the government came forward to contribute the share capital. With regard to borrowed funds, deposits are very meager and such cooperatives heavily depend on government borrowings and borrowings from cooperative banks.

### Management

As majority of the members of forest cooperatives are illiterate, managerial help is rendered by government by means of providing trained managers and personnel. The awareness of the members about the general body, board, etc., is very low. The success of forest cooperatives depends on the efficient and dedicated personnel.

### Operational Features

Forest cooperatives provide multi-purpose functions in the form of providing credit, marketing facilities, public amenities, extension education, etc., to the members. The forest cooperatives have coordination with nearest marketing cooperatives and sell the produces of the members through such cooperatives. Their input needs and consumer needs are also procured through such nearest marketing cooperatives. For their financial requirements, they depend heavily on government subsidies and financing by cooperative banks.

## Problems of Forest Cooperatives

1. *Illiteracy:* As majority of the members are illiterate, management of forest cooperatives is a great problem. In several countries, the management service is provided by the department of cooperatives as a special case. But continued dependence on government service makes them non-independent organizations.
2. *Remoteness of forests:* The forest cooperatives are located in remote forest, which distance them from transport and communication facilities. Only cluster of groups or communities are living in forest areas and to collect them under the fold of cooperatives is a difficult process.
3. *Moneylenders:* Like the fishermen, farmers and weavers, the members of forest cooperatives are also exploited by the moneylenders. These moneylenders not only exploit the forest people, but also illegally cut the trees through them and spoil the conditions of forests.
4. *Block capital:* Heavy investment is needed for construction of buildings, purchase of transport vehicles and to provide public amenities. Such investment cannot be mobilized from the members. Only institutional agencies can contribute such investments needed for the forest cooperatives.
5. *Poverty of members:* Savings from the members would be very low in such cooperatives. As the members are very poor and they make a livelihood under difficulties, savings would be very poor from them.
6. *Government regulations:* Government regulations in protecting the forests affect the development of forest cooperatives. In many countries, governments have enforced strict regulations in cutting the trees and extracting minor forest products.
7. *Illegal cutting of trees:* Rude exploitation of trees reflects the growth of forests and the working of forest cooperatives. The members are unable to collect forest

produces continuously. Steps must be taken to prevent the illegal felling of trees and degradation of forests.

8. *Funds:* The scope for processing activities, though high, is prevented want of funds. Processing cooperatives involve huge funds. Processing activities like honey making, extraction of herbal oils, etc. need heavy investment.

**Suggestions for Forest Cooperatives in Ethiopia**

Once, Ethiopia was having vast area of forestlands. Stage by stage these forests have been reduced due to illegal cutting of trees and cutting of trees for firewood. The government machinery was unable to check such practices due to the vastness of the forest areas. So, the time has come to protect the forests and safeguard the interest of agriculture by means of sustaining rainfall. There are forest cooperatives in Oromia region, SNNPR of Ethiopia, which are started by Farm Africa and other NGOs, and Cooperative Promotion Offices. The following suggestions are relevant to the forest cooperatives in Ethiopia.

1. Forest cooperatives have greater relevance to the highland people of Ethiopia. Highland people engaged the cultivation of coffee, tea, and teff. Due to the increase in population, encroachment on forests have become a feature. Through the organization of forest cooperatives, existing forest can be safeguarded and future growth of forests can be ensured.
2. Through the organization of forest cooperatives, employment opportunities can be created to population. Unemployment is growing and it is a problem to be tackled in the country. Forest cooperatives can provide full employment opportunities for the population by engaging in tree plantations, organized cutting of trees, collecting forest produces, and by developing forest nurseries.
3. Afforestation measures can be undertaken through forest cooperatives. Countries like Israel have shown that artificial forest can be created using modern agricultural

technology. The rainfall, climatic conditions, and soil conditions allow Ethiopia to go for growing more trees. This is possible through the forest cooperatives.

4. Soil erosion, which is a major problem for Ethiopia, can be handled properly by the forest cooperatives. The soil erosion should be stopped to keep the fertility of the soil. Through modern cultivation methods and technical advices, soil erosion can be reduced. This is possible through the forest cooperatives also.
5. Minor forest produces can be encouraged through forest cooperatives. Development of minor produces is quite absent in Ethiopia. Development of minor forest produces can provide employment opportunities to the population also.
6. Forest cooperative have also wider scope to export forest goods. Many developing countries, like Sri Lanka, are heavily depending on forest produces like tea and coffee for their export. Such crops can be developed and commercialized by the forest cooperatives in Ethiopia.

**Summary**

- Forest is an important wealth to a country because they are the primary source for rain. They control soil erosion and for the development of flora and fauna, forest is necessary. Forest provides lots of employment opportunities for the tribal population.
- The membership of forest cooperatives is confined to the tribal population and the people who are living in forest areas.
- Forest cooperatives provide marketing activities and other services to the members.
- In addition to the provision of credit, marketing, and service functions, marketing cooperatives undertake development activities like construction of forest roads, providing transport facilities, constructing community halls, controlling fire-fighting system, etc.

- Forest cooperatives are facing number of problems. They are away from the main land and transport and communication facilities are great problems.
- Illegal felling of trees and deforestation have become major problem, which affects the working of forest cooperatives.
- Ethiopia has enormous scope for the development of forest and forest cooperatives. The good rainfall and soil conditions are very conducive for the development of forest and forest cooperatives.

**Self-learning Activity**

Try to answer the following questions on your own:

1. Discuss the objectives of forest cooperatives.
2. What are the functions of forest cooperatives?
3. What suggestions can be given to forest coops in Ethiopia?

# 9 Irrigation Cooperatives

## Introduction

Irrigation cooperatives are one of the important cooperatives engaged in the development of agriculture and food security. They are also engaged in the process of water harvesting, water conservation, and judicious use of water for irrigation purposes. Cooperatives of this type are concerned with the supply and control of water for irrigation and drinking purposes also. In carrying out this function, they may:

1. Build and maintain dams, canals, ditches, and pipelines.
2. Pump water from streams, lakes, and rivers.
3. Clear and purify water for drinking purposes.
4. Provide piping, sprinklers, and other irrigation equipments for common use.
5. Establish and control water distribution system among the members.

## Types of Irrigation Cooperatives

Irrigation cooperatives have been organized in countries like U.S.A, China, India, etc. Irrigation cooperative are organized in riverbeds, lake areas and even in plain areas lifting irrigation from the ground water.

## Benefits of Irrigation Cooperatives

1. Irrigation cooperatives assured the guarantee of irrigation facilities throughout the year to the farmers. During the

times of rainy season, they store the water and supply them during off seasons. Irrigation cooperatives, like lift irrigation cooperatives get the ground water and supply them to members.

2. They conserve the water resources from the wastage. During the times of rainy season, water is wasted and such wasted waters are stored and used for future purposes. Through this process, they control soil erosion also.
3. Irrigation cooperatives provide employment opportunities to the small farmers. By means of undertaking intensive cultivation, small farmers take more crops and get full employment opportunity.
4. They contribute much to the agricultural prosperity and food security. By providing assured irrigation facilities, agricultural production increases and food security is assured.
5. In many countries, the rainwater is being wasted due to improper conservation measures. Irrigation cooperatives would be a boon to such areas.
6. They also teach the farmers about modern methods of agriculture and irrigation management. Irrigation cooperatives have employed technical experts and extension workers to undertake such functions.
7. They contribute to the intensive agriculture and increase the income of the farmers and keep the farmers engaged in agriculture throughout the year.

**Working of Irrigation Cooperatives**

The membership of irrigation cooperatives is confined to the farmers who own land. In irrigation cooperatives like lift irrigation cooperatives, the membership is confined to the members who are residing in a particular village or group of villages. In certain countries, governments construct small irrigation dams and handover the administration and maintenance to the irrigation cooperatives. Irrigation cooperatives need fixed capital for the purchase of irrigation pumps, construction works, etc. These long-term capitals are raised from external agencies like the financial institutions, government, etc. The success of irrigation cooperative depends on the help extended by the government in the form of providing irrigation sources, agricultural lands, irrigation instruments, etc.

## Irrigation Cooperatives in Ethiopia

Ethiopia is a land-locked country and irrigation cooperatives have been organized in lake areas. The purpose of forming such cooperatives is to distribute lands in lake areas for the unemployed youths and to provide sources of irrigation by erecting pump sets. In Ethiopia, irrigation cooperatives are not engaged in the construction of small dams, filter points, etc., like other countries. There is enormous scope for the organization of irrigation cooperatives in Ethiopia because the country has continuous rainfall for four months, which could be saved by irrigation cooperatives and can make the farmers to grow more than two crops a year.

At present, irrigation cooperatives cover only lake areas. On the other hand, highland areas, river basins and low land areas have also immense scope for the organization of irrigation cooperatives. It is to be noted that in Ethiopia only 5 per cent of the agricultural lands are getting assured irrigation facilities. By encouraging the irrigation cooperatives this percentage could be increased and food production and agricultural production can be increased tremendously.

## Problems of Irrigation Cooperatives in Ethiopia

1. Irrigation cooperatives need heavy investment, which is a major problem. They need lot of money and long-term finance to construct small dams, ponds, and to purchase irrigation equipments. Without strong financial basis, such activities cannot be undertaken.

2. Poor management led to the dormancy of many irrigation cooperatives. The initial enthusiasm of organizing the cooperatives fades away after few years. The members must see that they fully use the service of the irrigation cooperative forever.
3. Land scarcity is a problem to organize irrigation cooperatives. That is one of the reason that irrigation cooperatives are insisting that only landowners can become members of such cooperatives.
4. Government help is very much needed in the form of constructing minor irrigation projects. Construction of dams, ponds, drainage, canals, etc., are costlier and such activities must be undertaken only by the government.
5. Failure of monsoon, drought, etc., affects the working of irrigation cooperatives. During such times, the activities of irrigation cooperatives come to a halt.

**Summary**

- Irrigation cooperatives are one of the important cooperatives engaged in the development of agriculture and food security.
- Irrigation cooperatives are popular in countries like USA, Chin, and India. They are organized in rive beds, lake areas, and in plain areas.
- Irrigation cooperatives provide guaranteed irrigation facilities to the farmers. The small farmers are the important beneficiaries of irrigation cooperatives.
- The irrigation cooperatives purchase irrigation equipments like pump sets, drip irrigation instruments, etc., and hire them to the members.
- Ethiopia has enormous scope for the organization of irrigation cooperatives in lake areas.
- The major problems faced by irrigation cooperatives in Ethiopia are, lack of finance, dormancy of cooperatives, land scarcity, and lack of government help.

## Self-learning Activity

Try to answer the following questions on your own:

1. What is the current position of irrigation cooperatives in Ethiopia?
2. What are the problems faced by irrigation cooperatives?

# 10 Multi-Purpose Cooperatives

## Importance of Multipurpose Cooperatives

A cooperative society engaged in only one activity is called as single-purpose cooperative, and if a society undertakes more than one function, it is called as multi-purpose cooperative. The cooperative movement in many countries was started with single purpose cooperatives. But after the Great Economic Depression of the 1930s, emphasis was shifted to multipurpose cooperatives. The importance of multipurpose cooperative is great to farmers than the urban people. Multipurpose cooperatives are functioning well in countries like Japan, Germany, India, etc. On the other hand, single-purpose cooperatives are popular in Denmark and Holland. Multipurpose cooperatives are advantageous to the farmers. A multipurpose society is expected to undertake the functions of "better farming, better business, and better living".

Better farming denotes the provision of facilities like credit, inputs, etc. Better business denotes the undertaking of marketing activities, servicing activities, etc. Better living denotes the provision of incremental income to the farmers and providing all comforts to farmers.

The FAO, in its meeting held in 1949, pointed out the importance of multipurpose cooperatives as follows:

"It is believed that generally, in the rural areas, multipurpose societies fulfill a greater need and have a better change of success than single-purpose societies. In one institution they could meet the normal requirements of the agriculturalist. The volume of business would be large and overhead costs lower. The question of finding enough and suitable persons for management could also be more easily solved. Accordingly, in some member countries it is now the vogue to organize multipurpose societies and benefits derived there from have already been experience".

**Functions of Multipurpose Cooperatives**

The following are the multipurpose activities that can be undertaken by a village agricultural cooperative.

1. ***Provision of credit:*** A multipurpose cooperative can provide all three types of agricultural credit, namely short-term credit, medium-term credit, and long-term credit. Provision of credit is the important function of a village cooperative.
2. ***Provision of inputs:*** A multipurpose cooperative can provide agricultural inputs like improved seeds, chemical fertilizers, pesticides, etc. to the farmers.
3. ***Output marketing:*** Output marketing denotes the selling of agricultural produces of the farmers. Cooperatives are the better agencies to market the agricultural produces and give a better price to the farmers.
4. ***Providing consumer articles:*** A multipurpose cooperative can also provide consumer articles to the villagers, because in a village, farmers cannot get all the consumer articles and they have to go to the nearby city.
5. ***Encouragement of thrift and savings:*** A multipurpose cooperative must also provide savings facilities and provide banking facilities to the members.

6. *Service functions:* A multipurpose cooperative can also undertake service activities like hiring of agricultural machineries like tractor, sprayer, duster, etc.

They can also undertake transport facilities and insurance facilities to the farmers.

**Advantages of Multipurpose Cooperatives**

A multipurpose society has the following advantages and arguments are favored for their organization, due to the following factors:

1. ***Relationship between farmer and society:*** A multipurpose cooperative society can provide all types of service and supplies to the farmers in one place. This strengthens the relationship between the farmer and the cooperative society.
2. ***Less share capital contribution:*** If more number of single purpose cooperatives are there, farmers have to pay share capital to all the single purpose cooperatives. On the other hand, in a multipurpose cooperative society, by paying limited shares, they can get all services.
3. ***Cooperative potential:*** The cooperative potential among the members with regard to leadership, management, motivation, and enthusiasm will be very high in a multipurpose society because these energies are not shared by various single purpose cooperatives.
4. ***Cost of operations:*** The cost of operations in a multipurpose cooperative society will be very less per unit because the administrative cost will be reduced by means of spreading the cost to several activities.
5. ***Viability:*** A multipurpose society can run successfully and efficiently and can create viability. Viability means, to continue the operations successfully without any loss of business. The volume of business in one activity can be compensated to other activities if there is less volume of business.

6. ***Better personnel:*** A multipurpose cooperative can earn good profit and income. This will allow the society to appoint trained, experienced, and qualified managers and staff.
7. ***Spreading of risk:*** In a multipurpose cooperative society, the risk is spread over several activities. If there is loss in one business, that can be compensated in other businesses also.
8. ***Work throughout the year:*** A multipurpose society can engage itself in business operations and services to members throughout the year. But in the case of single purpose society, the operations may be limited to a particular season.
9. ***Mutual stimulation:*** In a multipurpose cooperative society, one activity stimulates other activities. Credit encourages production, production encourages marketing; marketing encourages processing, and so on. When income of the farmers increases, savings are also increased.
10. ***Combination of business activities:*** One of the preconditions for the success of farm operations is the linking of credit with marketing, processing, and consumer activities. As all these functions are undertaken by the multipurpose cooperative, the linking of business activities has become easier.
11. ***Mutuality among members:*** A multipurpose cooperative can bring the talents and mutual relations of the farmers in a village to a particular junction. The farmers can meet often and discuss their agricultural problems and the problems of the cooperative and solve it mutually.

**Disadvantages of Multipurpose Cooperative**

Though multipurpose cooperatives have number of advantages, they have certain limitations in their functioning.

1. ***Burden on the management:*** When the number of activities increases, the burden for the management also increases to make all the functions to run successfully.

2. ***Suitability of a manager:*** To find a suitable manager, who knows all the operations of a multipurpose society is very difficult. One can be "jack-of-all-trades but master in none".
3. ***Dispersal effect:*** When the number of activities are undertaken, a society cannot concentrate equally on all activities. Some activities may be neglected, which may affect the service of such activity.
4. ***Bookkeeping systems:*** To maintain the accounts of a multipurpose cooperative society is complicated. Separate records and account keeping must be maintained for each activity.
5. ***Cost calculation:*** When a society is undertaking many activities, it is very difficult to calculate the cost of operations of a particular business. Likewise, it is very difficult to find out the profit earned through a particular business.
6. ***Mixing trading and business:*** Marketing and credit functions should not be mixed with each other. There is all possibility to invest the short-term funds in long-term ventures, which may lead to the ultimate failure of the multipurpose cooperative.
7. ***Conflicting interest:*** In a multipurpose cooperative society, the membership will be very high. There may not be consensus among the members in running their cooperative and giving priority to the business operations. Such deferred interest may lead to conflict and failure of the cooperative.

In spite of the limitations of multipurpose cooperatives, they are suited to the developing countries, where the farmers are less educated and managerial talents to run the cooperatives is scarcely available.

**Factors the decided the Choice of Single-Purpose or Multipurpose Cooperative**

The following factors will help the farmers to decide a single purpose society or a multipurpose cooperative to their village.

1. ***Village size:*** If the size of the village is small and farmers are few in number, it is better to organize multipurpose cooperative society. On the other hand, if the village is big and the number of farmers is large, single-purpose cooperatives can be organized.
2. ***Degree of specialization:*** If the degree of specialization is high for a particular agricultural operation, like the processing cooperatives, it is better to organize single purpose cooperatives. On the other hand, if the degree of specialization is not technical, multipurpose cooperatives can be organized.
3. ***Structure of membership:*** If the population is high in the area with small farms, it is better to organize single purpose cooperatives. On the other hand, if the size of membership is small, multipurpose cooperative alone is suitable.
4. ***Management:*** To run a multipurpose cooperative society, trained and experienced manpower is needed.
5. ***Federal structure:*** When a strong federal structure is there, at the village level multipurpose cooperatives can be organized because federations can help the primary cooperatives in many ways.
6. ***Tradition in a country:*** Countries like Denmark and Holland have the tradition of organizing single purpose cooperatives. On the other hand, developing countries like India, China, Kenya, Nigeria, etc. have created the tradition of organizing multipurpose cooperatives.

**Summary**

- When a cooperative society is undertaking more than one function, it is called a multipurpose cooperative.
- Multipurpose cooperatives are organized mainly in villages, which undertake the functions of credit, marketing, processing, etc.
- Multipurpose cooperatives are suitable to the farmers because they can get all kinds of inputs, services, and other facilities in one focal point.

- At the same time, multipurpose cooperatives have certain limitations. Experienced manager is needed. The cooperative leaders must have enough experience and business techniques to run such cooperatives.
- In small villages, multipurpose cooperatives can be organized and in bigger villages, the single purpose cooperative can be organized. But in developing countries, only multipurpose cooperatives are suitable for the farmers.

**Self-learning Activity**

Try to answer the following questions on your own:

1. Discuss the importance of multipurpose cooperatives.
2. What are the factors that decide the choice of single or multipurpose cooperatives?
3. What type of cooperatives is suitable to Ethiopia: Single purpose or multipurpose?

# 11 Agro-Engineering Cooperatives

Agro-engineering Cooperatives are a type of rare cooperatives which are engaged in hiring and repairing agricultural machineries like tractors, harvesters, sprayers, dusters, etc. Through this process they provide all the needed agricultural machineries at a cheaper rate to the farmers. They are also engaged in the repair of the agricultural machineries of other cooperatives.

**Cooperative Use of Machinery**

In small-scale farming, it is not within the means of individual farmer to use his own machinery, and therefore, mechanization of agriculture, especially in underdeveloped countries, has not been very successful.

It is, therefore, advisable that the farmers may resort to the joint use of mobile machines. This will, however, depend on:

1. the structures of the farms;
2. the accessibility of the farms and the conditions prevailing; and
3. the existence of an efficient maintenance and repair service within a reasonable distance.

In case the cooperative society finds the joint use of machinery technically feasible, it will have to estimate the operating costs in reference to the expected revenue and will also have to keep in view the initial capital required to buy the machinery concerned. The joint use of machinery has been generally undertaken by multipurpose societies. In certain cases, single purpose societies, like agro-engineering cooperatives are also engaged in this activity. In the latter case, machinery pools have often been organized by small groups of members within the existing cooperatives, with their supervision and support. With a view to achieving the maximum profits it is necessary that the machines are used in the most efficient and effective manner and the operations are constantly supervised. For the efficient use of the machinery, it is necessary that the society obtains the maximum service from the machine and that it avoids empty operations.

## Operational Features of Machinery

### *Avoiding Empty Operations*

Empty operations of the machine can be avoided by:

1. clearly demarcating the area of operation before the start of the season and formulating the working plan. This will, obviously, require early registration of the members' demand for the machine service;
2. restricting the operators of the machines from using it for personal uses; and
3. planning the supplies of lubricating oil, diesel oil, etc. which should be delivered at the place of use of machines rather than taking the machine miles away to the petrol station. Again, proper maintenance of the machine is an important point to be kept in view.

## Maintenance

A high degree of maintenance not only keeps the repair costs to a minimum but also increases the life of the machine. This will require:

1. regular servicing and check-up;
2. annual overhauling; and
3. protection of the machine during off-season. Further, the society will have to engage experienced operators and

will also have to ensure that in no case the machine is left to be operated by the member himself. Lastly, the society will also have to ensure that operators avoid all risks that may damage the machine or equipment.

**Control of Machines**

For exercising a proper control on the operation of the machine, a number of points have to be kept in view.

1. Constant supervision will have to be carried out, the machine or equipment will have to be given only to trusted and competent staff member.
2. A log book regarding the use of the vehicle or the machine will have to be maintained, indicating the working time, the description of the work done, etc.
3. The amount to be charged from the members for the use of the machine has to be calculated in such a way that the cost of operations is fully covered. The charges may be calculated according to time, output and fuel consumption.
4. A part of the chargeable amount can be obtained in advance and the balance at a future date.
5. Non-members should be made to pay cash immediately after the operations are over.
6. It will also have to be ensured that no payments are made to the operator of the machine. The payments will have to be made either directly to the society or to an authorized person against a proper receipt.

**Special Features of Agro-engineering Cooperatives**

1. Agro-engineering Cooperatives have a wider area of operation to cover number of primary cooperatives, marketing cooperatives, and processing cooperatives.
2. They make heavy investment for the purchase of agricultural machineries.
3. They are engaged in the process of mechanization of agriculture, through which agricultural production is increased.

4. These cooperatives, usually do not admit individuals as members, on the other hand they admit only cooperatives as members.
5. These cooperatives have infrastructure facilities like repair stations, fuel stations, spare parts distribution, etc.
6. They are able to quicken the agricultural operations like, ploughing, weeding, and harvesting. As agricultural operations are seasonal in nature, they help to conduct such operations without any delay.

**Working of Agro-engineering Cooperatives**

The membership of Agro-engineering Cooperatives is confined to primary cooperatives, marketing cooperatives, processing cooperatives, etc., which are engaged in doing service and supplies to the farmers. Usually individuals are not admitted as members. Such cooperatives need heavy fixed capital which is contributed by the members and by making borrowings from other financial agencies.

**Problems of Agro-engineering Cooperatives**

1. The rate of dormancy is high among Agro-engineering Cooperatives because machineries used by such cooperatives are costlier and due to the non-availability of spare parts, machines are not used. The maintenance cost of such machineries is also very high.
2. These cooperatives are unable to function throughout the year due to the seasonal nature of agricultural operations because agricultural operations are seasonal in nature.
3. Repair and replacement works are not done effectively. Without having repair stations of its own, an agro-engineering cooperative cannot run successfully. Maintaining such workshop is a additional establishment. Likewise, the old machines must also be replaced frequently.
4. In areas, where agricultural labourers are concentrated, they put stiff resistance to such cooperatives, because their operations affect labourers employment opportunities in agriculture.

5. Replacing the old machines with new machines is a problem because it involves huge capital.

**Summary**

- Agro-engineering cooperatives are special types of cooperatives that are organized on a small-scale as well as wider scale.
- These cooperative are organized by the farmers to make use of agricultural machineries. Because small farmers do not have the capacity to purchase costly agricultural machineries.
- In countries like India, agro-engineering cooperatives are organized by primary cooperatives and they have wider area of operation.
- These cooperatives have to be careful in the use of machineries. The empty operations of machines must be avoided. Machines for personal use must be restricted.
- Maintenance of machineries is the most important aspect of agro-engineering cooperatives.
- Many agro-engineering cooperatives have their own workshops for repair and keep a stock of spare parts of machineries.
- One of the problems faced by such cooperatives is the dormancy. In the long run, after using the machineries, replacement of such machineries hardly takes place, which led to the dormancy of such cooperatives.

**Self-learning Activity**

Try to answer the following questions on your own:

1. What are the operational features of agro-engineering cooperatives?
2. What are the problems of agro-engineering cooperatives?

# 12 Fisheries Cooperatives

Like agriculture, industry, weaving, etc, fishing is also considered to be an important occupation. Countries with long coastal areas and highland countries have enormous fishing scope and in such countries fishing has become the main occupation for the people. Mechanization and technical advancements have been introduced in fishing and processing the fish. Many countries are exporting fish products, which is a major export earning for such countries. Fish is a nutritious food and it contains lot of minerals and nutrition needed for all age groups.

**Peculiarities of Fishery Industry**

1. Fishing industry involves lot of risks related to nature. Hence, production depends on natural conditions. During the times of cyclone, tsunami, etc, fishermen cannot go to the sea and their occupation is very much affected.

2. Weather is an important precondition for the success of fishing industry. The yield depends on temperature. Rough weather makes fishing difficult but also may cause damages to fishing boats and fisherman.

3. Fishing industry needs storage and processing facilities to make it a profitable industry. Without these facilities, fishermen cannot get value addition. For exporting of fish items, the above facilities are needed.

4. The fishing market is unorganized and price fluctuations are wider in the market. Like agricultural commodities,

during certain seasons the catchments will be high and during certain seasons the catchments will be very low.

5. Like the exploitation of farmers by the middlemen, fishermen are also exploited by middlemen and big boat owners. The fishermen do not have protected occupation and their income is instable, which are exploited by middlemen.
6. In many countries, fishing industry is unorganized and fishermen are unable to get financial help from institutional agencies. Only institutional agencies like fisheries cooperatives and banks can help the fishing industry to improve the technology and production.
7. The living conditions of the fishermen are not better than agriculturalists, and in many countries they have a poor standard of living. Due to the exploitation by middlemen and unstable income, the conditions of fishermen are very poor.
8. Like the small farmers in agriculture, small fishermen dominate in many developing countries. For such people, the only helping hand is provided by fisheries' cooperatives.

**Benefits of Fisheries Cooperatives to Fishermen**

1. Scattered fishermen are united by the cooperatives and they get lot of benefits out of cooperative efforts. Through the fisheries' cooperatives, their bargaining power is improved and many facilities are extended by the fisheries' cooperatives.
2. Huge capital is needed for the purchase of fishing needs, which can be provided by the fisheries cooperatives. Long-term capital is needed for the purchase of mechanized boats, erecting processing units, etc.
3. Cooperatives can provide loans for the purchase of boats (mechanized and modern). Small fishermen, who cannot operate modern boats, can purchase their own small-mechanized boats through cooperatives.

4. Cooperatives also provide fishing accessories like fishnets, fishing yards, etc. Fishnet is one item, which often gets spoiled and continuous repairing may not be useful. So, they have to purchase new fishnets very often.
5. Cold storage facilities are essential for modern fishing and that could be provided only by fisheries cooperatives. Fish, like milk, is a perishable commodity and the time to market is very much limited. To extend the life, cold storage facilities are always needed.
6. Processing facilities and facilities like salting, drying, canning, etc. can be provided by fisheries cooperatives. These facilities are needed to preserve the fish for a long period.
7. Value addition can be provided by fisheries cooperatives by means of engaging in the production of canned fish, fishmeal, fish oil, etc. For this purpose, heavy investment is needed to install processing units and fish oil extraction units.
8. Cooperatives provide a good marketing channel for the fishermen. This is one of the important functions undertaken by the fisheries' cooperatives. Through combined effort, they increase the bargaining power of the fishermen.
9. Supply of diesel, ice, salt, and equipments could be made at a cheaper price by the cooperatives. These are essential commodities for which shortage may arise at any time. So, cooperatives have to store these items and supply them regularly to the members.
10. Fishermen need insurance facilities for the loss and damage of boat, equipment, and the catch as well as life insurance, which could be provided by cooperatives.
11. Cooperatives can provide credit, savings, and banking facilities. These are certain multipurpose activities that are expected to be undertaken by the fisheries' cooperatives.

## Working of Fisheries' Cooperatives

### *Membership*

Individuals engaged in full time fishing can become members of fisheries cooperatives. Two types of fisheries cooperatives have been organized, one for the inland fishing and another for sea fishing. While admitting members, the cooperatives must be careful in avoiding master fishermen, who may exploit all the services of fishery cooperative.

### *Capital*

Fisheries cooperatives are in need of long-term capital (block capital) and short-term capital (working capital) like that of an industrial cooperative. Long-term capital is needed for the purchase of modern boats to the members and for the purchase of net and other fishing materials. Long-term capital is also needed for the construction of cold storages and processing units. Short-term capital is needed for the purchases of equipments and nets to the members. It is also needed for the distribution of credit to the fishermen. Fisheries cooperatives raise their finance from members and long-term finance is mobilized through cooperative banks and other banking organizations. In several countries, government contribution is also made for the purchase of fishing boats and fishing accessories.

### *Management*

The management body of fisheries cooperatives is the same like any other cooperative. The general body is the supreme authority and the board of directors work for the policy-making and administration. For the success of fisheries cooperatives, the board should have enlightened members with business and marketing skills.

## Problems of Fisheries Cooperatives

1. In seashore areas, fisheries cooperatives face the problem of damage due to natural calamities and cyclones. In

countries like Indonesia, such damages from nature are causing great loss to the fishermen and to the fisheries' cooperatives.

2. For a very long time fishermen were indebted to master fishermen and a system of bonded labor exist. This can be solved only by means of fisheries' cooperatives undertaking multipurpose functions of providing credit also.
3. Due to financial constraints, many cooperatives are unable to supply modern boats to the members. The investment cost needed to purchase boats, equipments, and processing units are costlier and cooperatives suffer due to lack of finance.
4. Recovery is a great problem for the fisheries cooperatives. In developing countries, fisheries cooperatives are facing this as a major problem.
5. Due to inefficient management, many fisheries coops have become dormant. Like small farmers, the fishermen are also least educated and they do not know to run their cooperatives. Managerial help during the initial stages must be extended by the government or the department of cooperatives.
6. Marketing is another significant problem of fisheries cooperatives. During the times of high price level, members never supply the fish catch to the cooperatives.
7. Government subsidy is an important factor for the successful running of fisheries cooperatives. Such subsidy has never been provided properly. So, in many developing countries, agriculturalists take priority in availing the government funds.
8. The success of fisheries cooperatives depends on the setting up of processing units, which have been neglected by many cooperatives. Without such processing units, value addition cannot be created and a fisheries' cooperative cannot run successfully.

1. The scope for organizing fisheries cooperatives in Ethiopia is limited to the lake areas.
2. As the size of population depending on fishing is negligible in Ethiopia, the number of fisheries cooperatives that could be organized is limited.
3. Fisheries cooperatives in the lake areas can be organized as an outlet of employment for the unemployed youth.
4. Several NGOs have experimented in organizing fisheries cooperatives in lake areas and they are running successfully.
5. As the priority the government is on food security, government has greater concentration on the promotion of agricultural and marketing cooperatives. Hence, the focus is not on fisheries cooperatives.
6. The hold of the private traders is strong over fish catching and marketing, any organization of fisheries cooperatives has to face stiff resistance from the private traders.
7. The government has to help in a big way for the organization of fisheries cooperatives in the form of providing long-term capital, technical help, processing facilities, and marketing facilities. Without government initiatives, fisheries cooperatives on a popular scale cannot be organized in Ethiopia.

## Scope for Organizing Fisheries Cooperatives in Ethiopia

### *Present Fishing Conditions in Ethiopia*

1. Ethiopia is landlocked country and hence, the fishing outlet is limited to lakes.
2. Lakes form the major part of inland fishing in Ethiopia.
3. River fishing is not popular in Ethiopia.
4. Unlike other countries, the population is not divided as fishermen in Ethiopia.
5. Fisheries cooperatives are practically non-existent in Ethiopia.

6. There is no institutional protection in the form of bank financing, government subsidy, etc. given to the fishery industry in Ethiopia.

## Summary

- In many countries where they have coastal areas, fishing has become an important occupation. Fishermen as special community are fully engaging in this industry.
- Like agriculture, fishing industry is also depending on nature and weather for its success. Fishermen like the small farmers are indebted to middlemen and they are exploited very much by the master fishermen.
- For small fishermen, to improve their living standards, the fisheries' cooperatives have become an important instrument. Fisheries' cooperatives provide credit and marketing facilities. They also supply boats and other fishing instruments needed for them.
- To manage fishing cooperative is a difficult thing because in many countries fishermen are illiterate like the farmers. The rate of dormancy is considerable in fisheries' cooperatives.
- Without government's help, fisheries' cooperatives cannot run successfully. Government has to provide subsidies for the purchase of mechanized boats, erecting processing units and for export market.
- Ethiopia has large number of lakes and the potential is very high to organize fisheries' cooperatives.

## Self-learning Activity

Try to answer the following questions on your own:

1. Discuss the benefits of fisheries cooperatives.
2. What is the scope for expanding fisheries cooperatives in Ethiopia?

# Part – II

## Management of Non-Agricultural Cooperatives

# 13 Housing Cooperatives

Dear learners! Before getting into study different types of non-agricultural cooperatives, you should have some knowledge about what of non-agricultural cooperatives is? After having an idea, we may proceed with housing and other non-agricultural cooperatives in the subsequent chapters.

**Non-Agricultural Cooperatives**

Non-agricultural cooperatives have been organized by non-agriculturalists. It doesn't mean that farmers cannot become members of such cooperatives and enjoy the benefits. In several countries, farmers are also admitted as members of non-agricultural cooperatives. The following are the features of non-agricultural cooperatives.

**Features of Non-Agricultural Cooperatives**

1. Non-agricultural cooperatives are organized mainly by non-agriculturalists.
2. They are organized mainly in urban areas and the main beneficiaries would be the urban population.
3. The capital involved for such non-agricultural cooperatives would be heavy.
4. The management of such cooperatives will be vested in the hands of educated population. Compared to the management of agricultural cooperatives, the management here would be efficient.

5. These cooperatives have to induct number of business techniques to improve their operational efficiency.
6. The competition from the private sector and government sector would be there for these cooperatives.

**Categories of Non-Agricultural Cooperatives**

The ILO in its working paper 19 divides non-agricultural cooperatives into three categories:

1. Cooperatives of industrial producers;
2. Cooperatives engaged in services, of which the members cooperative in the provision of facilities (such as transport cooperatives), as also in respect of cooperative engineering and so on;
3. Labour contracting cooperatives, which undertake works on behalf of their members and then have those works carried out on a team basis.

**Importance of Housing**

1. Next to food and clothing, the most important basic need for human beings is housing.
2. Due to the increase in population, the demand for housing also continues to grow.
3. Natural calamities, war, cyclone, tsunami, etc., led to construction of new houses.
4. Internal conflict, like that of African countries like Rwanda, Burundi, Sudan, Somalia, etc., increased the number of houseless refugees. Such people need housing facilities.
5. The growing middle class in developing countries led to the increase in housing facilities.
6. Increase in the level income in all countries led to the increasing need for housing.

**Housing Cooperatives**

Housing is a universal problem, next to food and clothing, the most important basic need for human beings is housing. Even highly prosperous countries cannot claim to have solved the problem of housing. In 1936, Theodore Roosevelt stated that about one-third of the nation was ill housed. In 1964, it was estimated that 25 per cent of the people in America still lived in substandard houses. But in developing countries, the housing problem has been aggravated by the population explosion. The Economic Commission for Asia and Far East, in 1967, while expressing great concern over the increase in urban population, strongly recommended to the governments in developing countries to accord high priority to housing programmes. The International Cooperative Alliance (ICA) recommended that cooperative housing should be given opportunities and support to continue its activity. The National Commission of Cooperative Development in USA stated that, in view of the failure of the private enterprise to cope up with the housing problem, "it becomes an obligation of the government or of the people themselves through cooperatives, to supply housing for those of limited economic means". In 1964, a Working Group on Housing Cooperatives in India pointed out that, "cooperative activity is the best means of providing decent houses at a reasonable costs to persons, particularly of low and middle income groups who cannot afford to satisfy their housing needs by their individual efforts". The ultimate objective of an individual in a civilized society is to own a house. But construction of houses involves heavy capital and it is beyond the capacity of an ordinary individual to construct his own house without external finance. Housing cooperatives are one of the prominent cooperatives in all types of economies.

Housing cooperatives played a significant role in solving the housing problems in foreign countries. In the period between two World Wars, more than half of the houses built in England were constructed with the help of housing cooperatives. Just before the Second World War one-fifth of the new buildings in Holland were built through housing cooperatives. In Sweden housing cooperatives were responsible for one-third of the new buildings constructed after the Second World War. The War devastated Germany;

housing problem was solved by housing cooperatives. In 1957 there were 1679 housing cooperative societies, constructed 6.8 lakh flats, which constituted 34 per cent of the total in Germany.

**Urban Housing Situations**

Due to increase in population, urban areas are facing the severity of the problem of housing. Such situations are explained below:

1. Rapid growth of population and rural-urban migration led to the pressure on urban housing situations.
2. Low-income level of majority of the households led to the housing shortages.
3. High costs relatively high standard of both public and private constructions became beyond the reach of urban households.
4. Scarcity and high prices of urban building lands, due to speculation led to scarcity.
5. Building regulations and related legislations tightened urban housings.
6. Inadequate provision of urban facilities and services made the urban housing situations worst.
7. Lack of saving and inadequate number of housing institutions led to pressure on urban housing.
8. Lack of coordination among various government authorities and urban planners led to the seriousness of housing problems.

**The Main Elements of Housing Cooperatives**

Though housing cooperative follow the principles of cooperation, they are different from other types of cooperatives. The main elements of housing cooperatives are as follows:

1. *Self-help:* Which does not necessarily imply manual self-help or renunciation of external help.

2. *Membership promotion:* Promotion of economic interests of the members through service relations between the members and the cooperative enterprise.
3. Identity of co-owners and customers of the cooperative
4. Democratic management and control of the society by the members and also equality of the members.

**Difference Between Housing Other Cooperatives**

Housing cooperatives are different from other types of cooperatives because:

1. The identity of producers (owners and co-owners) and consumers is particularly pronounced in housing cooperatives, as the members produce and consume one and the same commodity, i.e., house.
2. They require long-term planning, financing and organization in view of the cost and lifespan of house. This planning offers fewer possibilities for flexibility compared to other types of cooperatives. Wrong planning or inadequate financing could lead to dissolution or stagnation of the society.
3. Housing cooperatives usually depend on government and local authorities and also on their assistance particularly with regard to land acquisition and development, urban planning, financing, etc.
4. Human relations between the members and the urban community play an important role in the success or failure of the housing cooperative, because the members do not just work, produce, or purchase together, they also live together.

**Hesitation Reasons of Private Sector**

The private sector and the public sector have not come forward on a large scale to build houses for the middle class and low-income group. The private sector is hesitating to help them due to:

1. Scarcity and high cost of urban lands.

2. Inflexible or conservative attitude of lending institutions towards funding low-cost houses.
3. Administrative difficulties, particularly at planning and building permissions.
4. Managerial and administrative difficulties in the construction process.
5. Standards of construction and services are too costly.
6. The building materials used are beyond the reach of the target group.
7. Overheard costs and project administration costs are very high.

**Types of Housing Cooperatives**

Housing cooperatives have various organizational structure in various countries. We cannot find any uniformity in the organization of housing cooperatives like the agricultural cooperatives, consumer cooperatives or dairy cooperatives. Housing cooperatives can be broadly brought under two groups viz., operating agencies and financing agencies.

Under operating agencies, housing cooperatives build, buy or rent flats or houses to the members.

Under financing agencies, housing cooperatives arrange finance to the members.

**Functions of Housing Cooperatives**

The following subsidiary services are provided by the housing cooperatives:

*(a)* Community services and common facilities such as, garden, reading room, recreation centers, health centers, nursery schools, shopping centers, etc.

*(b)* Extension services to advice the members in all problems involving house building.

*(c)* Technical services such as design under drawing of building plans.

(*d*) Real estate services such as purchase and development of building plots and flats.

(*e*) Financing services such as providing finance and make convenient recoveries.

(*f*) Supply of building materials.

**Advantages of Housing Cooperatives**

1. Housing cooperatives could construct houses relatively at a cheaper cost because they go for bulk purchase of construction materials, which would become cheaper. The administrative cost and other overhead charges of housing cooperatives will be very reasonable.
2. The cost of construction has been brought down by the housing cooperatives through collective bargaining because the housing cooperatives purchase the housing plots even before a particular area is developed. Further, they get the construction materials at a cheaper cost due to bulk purchase.
3. Housing cooperatives have created new house owners and averted the exploitation of middlemen contractors. Majority of the housing cooperatives in many countries, including the developed countries, have helped the middle class and low-income group who cannot afford to purchase or construct a house instantly. They do not have such purchasing power to purchase a house within one time. For them, the only hope is housing cooperatives.
4. Housing cooperatives provide all technical, financial and material help for house construction. Primary housing cooperative have organized housing federations. Such housing federations provide technical, financial, and material help for the primary housing cooperatives. in several countries, separate housing financing banks have been established exclusively to finance the housing cooperatives.
5. New housing colonies, through housing cooperatives, are coming up with environmental friendly atmosphere.

Housing cooperatives have made it a point to go for the outskirt of a city and create housing colonies with natural atmosphere and clean environment.

6. Housing cooperatives undertake allied activities like road construction, drainage system, water connection, street lighting, etc. Housing cooperatives in the long run will not be content with construction of houses alone. They construct roads, drainage systems, water facilities, street lighting, and other welfare facilities.
7. The cooperative housing societies can exercise internal control to prevent speculation and illegal sale, subletting, or transfer of the house. Through its bylaws, the cooperatives can guarantee that the withdrawing member will sell or return the house to the society only.
8. The cost of construction and loan administration can be reduced by the housing cooperatives by running only one account. As a corporate body, the housing cooperative can secure construction loans collectively and obtain government and other public guarantees.
9. Through the collective repayment of loans and provisions for a reserve fund, the housing cooperative offers a system of mutual security, which can eliminate the danger of defaults.
10. The cooperative framework and organization enables collective maintenance and upkeep of houses, long-term planning of maintenance, and continued mobilization of members for the upkeep of their settlement.
11. Other facilities provided are as follows:
    *(a)* Architectural planning on a large scale;
    *(b)* Purchasing of housing flats at a cheaper price;
    *(c)* Obtaining building materials cheaply;
    *(d)* Fuller utilization of men and equipment on project basis;

(e) Planning, designing and construction of houses according to the approved standards and on collective basis; and

(f) Repayment of loans through installments and at the convenience of the members;

**Working of Housing Cooperatives Membership**

Housing cooperatives can be organized for different segments of population like rural and urban population, lower income group and middle income group, government servants and private sector employees, etc. There are various types of housing cooperatives like house construction cooperatives, housing finance cooperatives, etc. The membership of such housing cooperatives depends on the nature occupation, income, etc.

**Capital**

Housing cooperatives need huge finance because of the nature of house construction. The financing peculiarities of housing are as follows:

1. The nature of finance needed is long-term.
2. Owned funds of housing cooperatives are insufficient to meet the housing demand and they have to depend on external help.
3. The period of finance varies between 10 years to 30 years and above depending on the style of building and the nature of housing cooperatives.

Housing cooperatives raise their working capital from the members through share capital. But for long-term capital they depend on higher level (apex level) housing cooperatives, whose sole function is to raise long-term resources by means of issuing long-term debentures or long-term borrowing from government and other agencies.

**Recovery of Loans**

The disbursement of loans and the recovery of loans in housing cooperatives is different from other types of cooperatives. The loans are disbursed for a longer duration and the loan amount is collected through equal annual installments. In the case of fixed income groups and salary earners, the loan amount and interest are collected from their salaries. The housing finance cooperatives disburse the loan amount in two or three installments starting from above basement (the basement cost must be met by the member), roofing and final completion stage.

**Government and Cooperative Housing**

Governments are expected to promote and help the housing cooperatives because housing cooperatives solve the basic economic problem of the country. The following are the ways through which the governments must help the housing cooperatives:

1. Regulating the housing market by means of allocating housing plots to housing cooperatives at a concessional price.
2. Providing concessions to middle income group and lower income group in the form of subsidy to housing plot and construction cost.
3. Providing infrastructural facilities in housing cooperative areas in the form of constructing road, providing water facilities, lighting facilities, drainage facilities, etc.
4. Providing housing materials at a concessional rate to the housing cooperatives.
5. Providing long-term finance at a cheaper rate to the housing cooperatives.
6. Concession in house taxes for the houses constructed by housing cooperatives.

**Rural Housing and Cooperative Effort**

Rural areas have been neglected by the housing cooperatives because in rural areas the people do not have the purchasing power or repaying capacity. In the urban areas, the middle class consists of salary earners and they can afford to repay their loans in monthly installments, which is not possible for the rural population. The main difficulties in the execution of rural housing programmes through cooperatives are as follows:

1. Lack of consciousness among the villagers to improve their housing conditions and their reluctance to leave the ancestral houses.
2. Their inability to furnish collateral security for house-building loans.
3. Their ignorance of legal formalities and technical know-how.
4. Their ability to manage housing cooperatives is comparatively poor than the urban members.

**Problems of Housing Cooperatives**

1. *Lack of finance:* Housing cooperatives need long-term finance and ever growing housing need make them unable to meet the financial needs. Specialized agencies are needed to finance the housing cooperatives or housing schemes.
2. *Lack of housing federations:* The success of primary housing cooperatives depends on the federal housing cooperatives, whose main responsibility is to raise long-term resources and disburse them to the primary cooperatives.
3. *Scarcity of land and building materials:* With the growth of population, urban lands are becoming costlier and scarce. Year after year the cost building materials is also increasing.
4. *Neglect of rural areas:* Housing cooperatives have completely neglected the rural population, as they do not have the repaying capacity for the construction of costly houses.

**Scope for Organizing Housing Cooperatives in Ethiopia**

1. In Ethiopia, urban population is increasing and migration from rural areas is taking place fast. So, urban housing has become an urgent problem, which could be solved by organizing housing cooperatives.

2. Addis Ababa city, one of the largest cities in Africa, is getting pressurized for housing accommodation. If enough attention is not given to the housing problem, this city may become a slum. It is the right time to organize large number of housing cooperatives in Addis Ababa city.
3. The municipal governments are unable to provide civic amenities like road, communication, drinking water, etc. Some of these challenges could be met by means of organizing housing cooperatives.
4. Some of the big cities in Ethiopia are getting polluted due to improper town planning, invasion of rural population, and pressure over existing public amenities. These could be partially solved by organizing housing cooperatives.
5. The typical middle class is emerging in Ethiopia. They have affordable monthly income to pay for their own house taking a longer period of time. Such middle class can organize housing cooperatives and can have their own secured houses.

**Summary**

- Cooperative housing comes under non-agricultural cooperatives, and these cooperatives are very developed in northern countries.
- Due to the increase in population and urbanization, cooperative housing is gaining greater importance in developing countries also.
- The growing housing needs of countries could be solved by housing cooperatives.
- Housing cooperatives are not only providing houses to the members but also they undertake social amenities like road construction, water facilities, street lighting, etc.
- The working of housing cooperatives is different from other types of cooperatives. They need long-term finance

to construct houses and the recovery of loans from members must be made only through installments.

- For the successful working of housing cooperatives, governments' help and concession are needed in the purchase of housing plots, tax concessions, registration fee, etc.
- Rural housing is one of the neglected areas and that could also be solved by housing cooperatives.
- In Ethiopia, housing cooperatives are not popular but there are growing opportunities to organize housing cooperatives to the urban middle class.

**Self-learning Activity**

Try to answer the following questions on your own:

1. Explain the advantages of housing cooperatives.
2. What are various types of housing cooperatives?
3. Discuss the scope for popularizing housing cooperatives in Ethiopia.

# 14 Consumer Cooperatives

A consumer cooperative is a voluntary organization of consumers, organized to obtain their requirements of consumer goods and services on terms of greatest advantage to them. This type of cooperative undertakes retailing, wholesaling and sometimes, the production and processing of consumer goods.

Most consumer stores have been established on the principles enunciated by the Rochdale Pioneers. These principles are: open membership, democratic control, and cash trading at market prices, fixed return on capital and dividend on purchases.

The main object of a consumer store is to serve its members and customers with goods required by them for household consumption. It is expected to provide goods at reasonable price and to protect the interest of the members. These stores are also expected to stabilize the price line and check the exploitation of the consumers by the private business.

The main achievements of consumer cooperatives are:

1. Reduction in costs of retailing with advantages accruing to consumers, thus making possible more savings and higher standard of living and contributing to economic stability.
2. Provision of better quality goods.
3. Promotion of thrift and consequent increase in economic security of members.

4. Education in intelligent buying, family budgeting and general economics.
5. Check on monopoly by cooperative competition and profiteering.

Consumer cooperatives are one of the important cooperatives found in almost all countries. Consumer cooperatives work for the welfare of the consumers by means of providing pure goods at reasonable prices and relieve the consumers from the exploitation of middlemen. The very cooperative movement was organized first in the field of consumer cooperatives by the Rochdale Pioneers of England.

**Need for Consumer Cooperatives**

1. Consumer cooperatives help the consumers from the exploitation of merchants. The hold of the private traders in consumer business is very strong. There are very many intermediaries between the producer and the consumer. They take away a portion of the price paid by the consumer and exploit the consumers. This is avoided by consumer cooperatives.
2. They provide pure and unadulterated goods. Since the days of Rochdale Pioneers, consumer cooperatives have made it a point to provide only pure and unadulterated goods. Quality consciousness is always with the consumer cooperatives.
3. Consumer cooperatives distribute the articles for a lower price than market price because consumer cooperative go for bulk purchase of commodities through their wholesale stores. The wholesale stores purchase the commodities at the production center or manufacturing centers and distribute them at a low margin to the primary cooperatives. In turn the primary cooperatives sell the goods for a lower price.
4. They help to bring down the market price. Market price is influenced mainly by the private traders. Wherever the number of consumer cooperatives is high, they are able to bring down the market price also.

5. Consumers are able to get all items in one place. The organization of departmental stores or supermarkets by the consumer cooperatives made it convenient for the consumers to get all the goods at one place.
6. Bulk purchase and purchase at production centers provide the economies of scale. Consumer cooperatives go for huge volume of purchase and the benefit is transferred to the consumers.
7. During the times of scarcity, they help the free flow of goods at a reasonable price. Cooperatives are not profit-oriented organizations and in many countries to distribute the essential consumer goods, governments have authorized them as the sole agency. Consumer cooperatives avoid the scarcity by means of keeping enough stock to the consumers.

**Working of Consumer Cooperatives**

There are various types of consumer cooperatives. Specialized consumer cooperatives are meant for ordinary consumers, factory workers, employees, and students. Consumer cooperatives are also classified as rural and urban consumer cooperatives. The membership of consumer cooperatives is open to all types of people but the consumer cooperatives for workers, employees and students, the membership is confined to that category of people. Ordinary consumer cooperatives and cooperative supermarkets serve the non-members also.

Consumer cooperatives operate through federal set-up. At the lower level, primary consumer cooperatives and cooperative supermarkets are there. At the district and regional level cooperative wholesale stores (UK Model) operate. At the regional level or national level consumer federations function. The function of the wholesale stores and the federations is to purchase consumer goods in bulk quantities and supply them to the primary stores. In several countries apex consumer societies are engaged in manufacturing of consumer goods. For example in Sweden, the KF (National Federation of Consumer Cooperatives) is engaged in manufacturing of consumer articles.

*Why the consumer co-operatives must apply management techniques?*

1. Consumer co-operatives have come to occupy a significant place in our distributive system. In all our national schemes priority has been given to the Consumer Cooperatives.
2. The importance of consumer co-operatives will long last only when they increase their competitive power. To compete with the private traders, the stores must enhance their quality of service by applying scientific principles of management.
3. The volumes of transactions handled by stores have been going on increasing year after year. The quantity must justify quality also. Better management will ensure quality of foods and service.
4. Consumer Co-operatives have been branded as the stabilizers of price level. They can check the erratic upward trend of price level. This has been amply proved by many of the Consumers' Co-operatives and Super Bazaars in various parts.
5. To modernize their service techniques and to promote the loyalty of the consumers, the stores have to introduce scientific techniques of management.

**Areas for Modern Management**

The Consumers' Co-operatives can introduce the modern management techniques in the areas of merchandising, sales promotion, inventory management, financial management and personnel management.

**I. Merchandising**

Merchandising includes the activities of purchasing, storage, stock taking, assortment, packaging and selling.

### 1. *Purchasing*

Prudent purchasing policies can take the stores to new successes and new vistas of promotion. Many of the stores failed due to their wrong sales policies. The following policies must be followed by the stores in purchasing commodities.

1. Goods must be purchased at the place where they are produced or manufactured. Small stores can purchase through their apex stores.
2. Goods must be purchased at right quality. Quality maintenance is a factor to keep up the patronage of the customers.
3. Goods must be purchased at right quantity also. Based on the previous movement of goods, goods must be purchased. Goods should not lie in stocks, which is equal to that locking of capital.
4. Goods must be purchased at right price also. As the stores have to compete in the market, they have to purchase the goods at a price keeping in mind the margin to be retained, competitor's price and to cover the establishment.
5. Goods must be purchased at a right time also. Harvest time is the best season to purchase agricultural commodities. Goods can be purchased when the liquidity position of the stores is sound. When stock is low purchases can be made.

In addition to the above principles, a store must know the type of customers for a product, the demand at a given time and normal or average sale of a particular commodity. The society must also decide the source of supply. To a larger extent they can depend on the wholesale stores, who in their turn indulge in bulk purchases thereby bring economies in purchasing.

### 2. *Stock Management*

Stock taking is undertaken periodically in stores. The stock is taken once in a month or once in three months or six months. The purpose of stock taking is to decide the actual value of stocks on hand and to prepare the profit and loss accounts and Balance Sheets. It is also needed to ascertain the shortage and to detect pilferage. It is also essential to know the slow sellers, fast sellers and stagnant items.

The stock must be taken after business hours and the stores must not be closed as it may lead to loss of confidence of the customers. To take the stocks a committee consisting of few board of Directors and employees must be formed. The committee must look after the following:

1. Check that all goods are price marked.
2. Measure the goods in terms of their weight or length or quantity.
3. Damaged goods and unsold goods must be sorted out separately.
4. Empty bags/boxes must also be counted as they can be sold.

**3. *Pricing***

Since the days of the Rochdale Pioneers, the consumer co-operatives have been following a cautions and notable policy. The stores have been able to distinguish themselves from others mainly out of following prudent price policy:

Goods can be sold at: (a) market price; (b) below market price; and (c) at above the market price. As the latter two policies are undesirable, the stores can follow the first one and must influence the market price. It can bring down the market price by following 'active price policy'. (Active price policy means, selling the goods below market price.) The pricing policy of consumer's stores is decided by the following factors:

1. The end price must be comparable and acceptable to the consumers.
2. Costs of the goods must be covered out of that price.
3. The stores must earn a margin to manage its overheads.

The following aspects decide the retail price:

1. Cost price of the commodity.
2. Risks in handling the particular article
3. The competition that prevails
4. The type of sales-system-prices can be reduced when self-service exists.
5. Nature of articles - for quick sale goods margin can be reduced.
6. The quality of service.

In cooperative stores, the Board must decide the fixation of prices. The Manager must help in working out the cost price and detailing the trends in marketing price.

**4. *Assortment***

Assortment means the sorting of goods into various groups for the convenience of the customers. Assortment can be divided into:

1. *Convenience Goods:* Goods that are often used by the consumer. These items are 'Quick Sale' items.
2. *Shopping Goods:* The values of these goods are higher and they are 'slow sellers'.
3. *Specialty Goods:* These goods are seldom purchased. Some times they become dead stock.

**Determination of Assortment**

1. Nature of the customers, their number and income.
2. Type of Competitions.
3. Average demand for capital of different goods.
4. Buying habits of the customers.
5. Location of the stores.
6. Selling system — self service, home delivery.
7. Availability of space and finance.

## II. Sales Promotion

Under the competitive setting, the consumer cooperatives have to enhance their sales promotion in order to increase their volume of transactions and to attract more customers. In other words sales promotion means:

1. Improving the turnover or business of the stores.
2. Creating interest among the customers.
3. To distinguish the stores from other competitors.
4. Introducing courtesy and keenness on the needs of the customer out of better service.

**Advantages of Sales Promotion**

1. Sales promotion increases the business turnover.
2. It attracts new customers and maintains the loyalty of old customers.
3. It fetches competitive service and price attraction.
4. It ensures steady sales; thereby sound financial flow is maintained.

***Criteria for Effective Sales Promotion***

1. The stores must display variety of goods.
2. The atmosphere to purchase in the stores must be calm and conducive.
3. Price information and commodity information must be provided.
4. Courteous service of the employees and their polite behaviour.
5. New ideas and innovative sales promotion techniques.

**Sales Promotion Aids**

For promoting the sales the stores have to use lot of sales promotion aids and techniques. The purposes of such aids are to improve the sales, to give proper price and commodity information.

The following aids are used to promote sales.

1. *Newspaper Advertisements:* This can be used during the time of festival seasons.
2. *Leaflets:* When new branches are organized or when new items are added, the customer can be informed of the activities of the stores out of this.
3. *Cinema Slides:* In cities and town, this aid will be very effective.
4. Window display.
5. *Meeting the Customer Directly:* This can be done during the times of general body meetings.

***Salesmanship***

Closely connected with sales promotion is salesmanship. Salesmanship is an effort to increase the efficiency of the salesman and to guarantee 'Customer attraction'.

Right type of sales force could be selected even during the selection. After the selection they must be given effective training.

Salesmanship is counted during the following functions of purchasing:

1. *Delivery of goods:* Right goods must be delivered.
2. *Quantity:* Right quantity must be supplied.
3. *Quality:* Quality goods must be supplied.
4. *Totaling the items:* Overcharges in the total must be avoided.
5. *Service complaints:* Complaints made by the customers must be looked after properly.

To promote the salesmanship weekly meetings of various sectors heads and meeting with their respective salesmen must be converted. Sales targets must be fixed and incentives can be given to the salesmen who have achieved the targets. Action must be taken over the salesmen who are indifferent to the customers.

## III. Inventory Management

Inventory management is an important area of consumer cooperatives management and it is the indicator to decide the customer service and profit. Inventory is the single largest item in the asset side of the Balance Sheet of stores.

### Importance of Inventory Management

1. Inventory management is the indicator, which shows the flow of goods.
2. Quick sales, slow sellers and dead stocks could be identified.
3. Better inventory system avoids locking of capital and ensures the liquidity of the stores.
4. Unwanted goods could be eliminated and new products could be introduced to customers.
5. Better inventory management could ensure needed brands with sufficient quantities.
6. Shortages of commodities averted and thereby hoarding are curtailed. Artificial scarcity is eliminated in the market.

#### *Purchase Budget*

The store must prepare purchase budget well in advance based on the previous sales. This must be approved by the Board. The goods must be purchased well before the stock depletes. A right level of inventory must be maintained. The technique of forecasting the demand must be effectively used. Better inventory must be maintained during the times of festivals, marriage seasons, and the first week of the month.

#### *Storage*

The goods that are purchased in lump must be stocked safely and proper accounts must be maintained.

### Pre-Requisites of Good Storage

1. Sufficient space is necessary to stock the goods purchased in bulk.
2. Right type of storage equipments must be maintained.

3. Protection from foreign elements must be ensured. The godown must be rat proof and fire proof.
4. The employees who handled the loading and unloading must be given sufficient training.
5. Pre-packing can be introduced.
6. Price making must be made on all items.
7. Separate shelves must be allotted for various goods.
8. Separate godowns or storing places must be arranged for explosives, fireworks, vegetables and medicines.

As the practice of 'double compartmental system' is common it can be scientifically perfected. This is possible by means of the proper maintenance of 'Purchase, Issue and Stock Register'. A percentage of allowance must be made for spoilage, pilferage, and leakage of goods.

***Inventory Checking***

Periodic checking over the inventories must be made. Stock verification can be made in a month or once in a quarter. This can avoid pilferage and shortages. The level of inventory to be maintained will also become easier out of periodic checking.

***Rate of Stock Turn***

Stock turn is the speed at which the inventory is exhausted by quick sales. Quick stock-turn is ensured for fast selling items. The profit-earning capacity of stores is determined by the number of times the stock is turned out.

On no account the stores must keep the dead stocks. Because dead stocks are a burden to the inventory and they will increase the loss. As far as possible, dead stock must be disposed. Selling them even below their fixed price is recommended instead of keeping them idle.

## IV. Financial Management

Like any other cooperatives, consumer cooperatives need fixed capital and working capital. But stores need more amount of working capital, which can be mobilized from members, other cooperative banks, etc. An efficient inventory management must be followed to avoid locking of capital.

Consumer cooperatives are in need of heavy working capital. As the working capital is short-term in nature, they borrow from cooperative banks and commercial banks. Primary stores used to get the commodities for credit from the federations. So they are not in need of large amount of working capital.

### V. Personnel Management

A consumer cooperative store needs efficient and trained personnel. Various section heads must be appointed for the areas of purchasing, stocking, inventory, sales promotion, etc.

### Areas Need Attention in Consumer Cooperatives

The consumer cooperative movement has not been able to make much headway. It has so far not succeeded in acting as 'price- setter in the market and has not made any significant contribution to 'holding the price line'. The consumer stores are suffering from a number of structural, operational, and administrative weaknesses. Most of these weaknesses have arisen as a result of their accelerated unplanned growth. Some of the important factors, which retarded the sound growth, and working of the consumer cooperatives in developing countries, including Ethiopia, are as under:

1. *Indifference of the state/regional government*

   The biggest single factor accounting for the poor performance was the apathetic and indifferent attitude of the government for a long time. Supplies to the stores were not regular and preference was given to private agencies, members of the cooperatives suffered on that account.

2. *Narrow basis of operation*

   One flagrant defect of these stores is the narrow basis of their operations. Most of them deal in limited number of commodities and hence the customers are not in a position to get most of their requirements from the store.

3. *Small and Uneconomic Sizes*

Most of the primary stores have been very small and non-viable units. They have poor membership; inadequate working capital and their average sales have been so low that they could hardly meet their ordinary expenditure. On account of their uneconomic size most of them were not making profits or were incurring losses.

4. *Inadequacy of Funds*

Lack of adequate finance has been another important handicap in the working of the stores. Most of the primary stores failed to collect large amounts of share capital and banking institutions did not oblige them with funds, as they had no faith in the efficient working of these stores.

5. *Lack of Efficient Management*

Most of the stores are manned by persons who have had hardly any experience of business. On account of the inefficient management the cooperative stores could not compete with private retail traders who are generally so well versed in the art of managing their small unit.

6. *Lack of Loyalty on the part of members*

The success of a cooperative store depends upon the unflinching and continuous loyalty of its members. However, the members of the store have not shown this loyalty. Most of the members patronize the store so long as their prices are lower than those of the market. Even at the same price they have not shown any preference to the stores.

7. *High Cost of Management*

The high cost of management has been another factor for the failure of the store movement. The private trader is free from a number of overhead expenses, which are so common in most of the consumer stores. A private trader thus enjoys many relative advantages over the consumer stores.

8. *Lack of link with other Cooperative*

   The consumer's cooperatives have not established any link with producers and marketing cooperatives. The consumers store also does not make purchases from the marketing and other cooperatives.

9. *Dishonesty of the Employees and Management*

   Some of the stores have come to the grief because of the dishonesty of their employees. No action was taken against the employees who had misappropriated the store money. In efficiency; red-tapism, nepotism, and corruption have crept into the vitals of some of the stores.

10. *Defective Price and Purchase Policy*

    Some of the stores had not followed a sound price and purchase policy. In planning and formulating these policies power is exercised by the chairman or secretary or the executive officer alone or in consultation with one another. The lack of proper purchase policy has been responsible for heavy losses in many of the stores.

In short following factors can be held responsible for causing losses to the consumer stores:

1. Adverse price fluctuations in agricultural commodities;
2. High overhead costs;
3. Low margin of profits;
4. Running small and uneconomic commodities;
5. Dealing mainly in controlled commodities;
6. Injudicious purchases;
7. Mismanagement and misappropriation; and
8. Locking up of funds in slow moving and un-saleable articles.

**Problems of Consumer Cooperatives**

1. Disloyalty of members is a great problem for the consumer cooperatives. Members go to consumer cooperatives when there is scarcity and the price is low. Other times, they go to the private shops.

2. Raising of working capital is another problem for consumer cooperatives. Many of the cooperative banking institutions are meant for agricultural cooperatives and there is no separate cooperative financing agency for consumer cooperatives.
3. They have to work under stiff competition from private traders. Private traders join together and sometimes try to weaken the consumer cooperatives.
4. In several countries, the absence of federal consumer cooperatives has weakened the position of consumer cooperatives. Federal cooperatives are needed for bulk purchases, to provide training, to guide the primary stores and to raise resources.
5. In developing countries government interference affects the working. Consumer cooperatives are compelled to distribute scarce consumer goods for a lower price.
6. At national level, consumer cooperatives must enter into the production of consumer articles and processing of food articles.
7. Personnel efficiency is also questionable in consumer cooperatives. The employees of consumer cooperative must be given continuous training in customer attraction and improving their working.
8. Lack of integration between consumer cooperatives, producers' cooperatives and marketing cooperatives.

**Suggestions for Improvement**

1. Primary store should aim at providing variety of goods and serving larger interest of members. This should depend upon local conditions and the needs of consumers.
2. Consumer stores should make bulk purchases through appropriate cooperative agencies.
3. Important consumer stores should undertake processing activities like oil-extraction, flour making, etc.
4. Government should give positive preference to consumer stores in the matter of granting import licenses.

5. Credit sales should be undertaken only by institutional stores where there is an agreement between the store and the employer that the credit amount due to a member would be deducted from his salary.
6. Consumer stores should pay patronage dividend on the basis of the purchases.
7. These stores should lay special emphasis on suitable purchase and price policy.
8. Consumer stores should introduce home delivery services to stimulate sales.
9. The stores should pay special attention to the quality of goods.
10. The stores should make bulk purchases and establish direct contacts with reputed manufacturers for securing wholesale agencies.
11. The board of directors should consist of persons who have some business experiences and who can inspire confidence in the public. All the staff of the store should be properly trained.
12. Salesmen should be induced to promote sales by offering them commission on sales, exceeding a certain minimum limit.
13. A proper system of supervision and checking should be introduced.
14. Managers should be given full freedom to carry out the policies laid down by the board of directors.
15. Stress should be laid on the importance of prompt and correct maintenance of accounts and audit.

**Summary**

- Consumer cooperatives are the oldest cooperatives in the world and they are organized almost in all countries.
- War, shortage of consumer articles, and price rise led to the organization of consumer cooperatives.

- In countries like England, Sweden, and other European countries, consumer cooperatives have established strong roots.
- In developing countries, there is need to organize large number of consumer cooperatives to eliminate the exploitation of middlemen, to control the price level, to provide pure goods to the consumers, etc.
- Consumer cooperatives are in need of applying modern management techniques in order to compete with the private sector and to do efficient services to the consumers.
- The areas that need the application of modern management in consumer cooperatives are merchandizing, sales promotion, inventory management, financial management, and personnel management.
- The major causes for the poor performance of consumer cooperatives in developing countries are lack of finance, lack of federal organizations, lack of efficient personnel, and lack of government support.
- To improve the working of consumer cooperatives in developing countries, the loyalty of the members must be improved; the working capital must be improved; wholesale stores must be organized; employees must be given continuous training; and link with other cooperatives must be created.

**Self-learning Activity**

Try to answer the following questions on your own:

1. Discuss the need to apply management techniques in consumer cooperatives.
2. What is the purchasing policy of consumer cooperatives?
3. Why do consumer cooperatives go for sales promotional efforts?
4. What suggestions can be given to improve working of consumer cooperatives?

# 15 Industrial Cooperatives

Industrial cooperatives are organized by unemployed people, village artisans, technicians, etc. In some countries they are called as producers' cooperatives also. Industrial revolution had resulted in the growth of large-scale industries and mass production. This posed a challenge to the small-scale industries. The original home of industrial cooperatives was France and it was Buchez, a disciple of Saint Simon, the popular cooperator, was responsible for the establishment of cooperative workshop in that country. In England in 1882, a cooperative production federation was established. Good progress has also been made in industrial cooperative in countries like, Italy, Russia, China and Japan.

**Definition**

"An industrial cooperative is an undertaking of craftsmen or skilled workers engaged in the cottage or small-scale industries to undertake production, purchase of supplies and raw materials, marketing of products and supplying other services to members".

**Objectives of Industrial Cooperatives**

Industrial cooperatives are organized with social and economic objectives. Among the social objectives, the important activity is to safeguard the interest of the poorer sections against exploitative trends and the dispersal of wealth. The economic objective of these societies is to create employment opportunities, increase in production, and create competitive capability and acceleration in the rate of capital formation. The bylaws of industrial cooperatives provide the following objectives:

1. To purchase and supply the raw materials, tools and equipments needed by the members.
2. To market the finished products.
3. To borrow funds from members and non-members.
4. To obtain contracts from government, public bodies, and others and to get them executed through the members.
5. To purchase and own machineries for being hired to the members.
6. To impart or arrange business and technical training to the members.
7. To grant advances to members on the security of raw materials and finished products belonging to them.

**Advantages of Industrial Cooperatives**

1. The main advantage of industrial cooperatives is to provide employment opportunity to the unemployed workers and artisans. With the globalization and privatization, the unemployed youth found it difficult to get reasonable jobs and for them industrial cooperatives are very useful.
2. They provide the bulk purchase of raw materials, equipments and tools. The needed raw materials are purchased in bulk and are distributed to members. Needed machineries and equipments are hired to the members.
3. They provide marketing facilities for the finished products. This is the most important function undertaken by industrial cooperatives. They open market outlets in important cities and sell the products and in certain cases they sell them in the open market.

4. They help to keep the traditional cottage and village industries survive. Cooperatives like weavers' cooperatives are providing lot of employment opportunity to the villagers and the traditional weaving is safeguarded and improved by the weavers' cooperatives.
5. They help to industrialize the nation by using the locally available raw materials. One of the peculiarities of industrial cooperative is to use the locally available raw materials. If raw material is not available nearby, they are purchased in bulk from outside and distributed to the members.
6. They provide regular employment and permanent income to the members. With the provision of better marketing facilities, regular flow of sales is assured to the members. This makes them to be engaged continuously in production, which gives them regular income.
7. Cooperatives like sugar cooperatives and processing cooperatives fulfill the essential commodity needs of the country. Likewise, industrial cooperatives organized in rural areas like the weavers' cooperatives, artisans' cooperatives, etc. meet the clothing and such other needs of the population.
8. Industrial cooperatives make an ordinary member to an entrepreneur. They not only stop with giving a regular income, but also in due course a share in the profit is given to the members through which they improve their living standards.

**Kinds of Industrial Cooperatives**

Industrial cooperatives have been organized in the fields of weaving, handicraft, transport, fishing, spinning, sugar, tea and coffee processing, etc. Industrial cooperatives are also classified under various categories like, workshop cooperatives, industrial service cooperatives, common facility cooperatives, etc. Like other types of cooperatives, industrial cooperatives have also federal structure starting from the primary level to national level. The regional and national federations are arranging marketing facilities and finance to the primary cooperatives. In several countries, industrial cooperatives are engaged in the export of industrial products.

**Classification of Industrial Cooperatives**

Industrial cooperatives can be classified under two categories, namely cooperative, which undertake production of goods and cooperatives, which undertake the supply and services. Under the first category, the production activity is carried out either in the house of the members or in a common workshop or factory. The members are supplied with raw materials, designs and specifications of goods to be produced, facilities for production and financing, etc., by the society. The marketing activities are also undertaken by the society. The members are paid only wages on monthly basis or on piece basis.

Under the service cooperative type, the members are provided with various types of services like raw materials, tools and equipments, technical guidance, etc. The members are also provided with marketing of the finished products. The society does not undertake the risk of production. The society is responsible only for providing services required by the members while the risk involved in production of the finished products is entirely of members.

Another classification of industrial cooperatives can be made as follows:

*Workshop cooperative societies*

Here, the members are given raw materials and the members have to produce the finished product and give it to the society for marketing. So, the society undertakes the supply of raw materials and marketing.

2. *Industrial service cooperative societies*

This type of society provides services like supply of raw material, marketing, etc. But they do not undertake the risk of production.

3. *Common facility workshop societies*

   Under this type, the cooperative construct workshops and members avail the services in the workshop and the products are sold by the cooperative.

**Working of Industrial Cooperatives**

***Membership***

Any unemployed individual and craftsmen who are in need of facilities can join the industrial cooperatives and avail the facilities and benefits provided by the industrial cooperatives.

**Capital**

Industrial cooperatives are in need of heavy finance of long-term nature for the purchase of machineries, equipments, construction of buildings etc. To provide long-term capital in several countries separate industrial cooperative banks exist.

**Business Activities**

Depending on the type of industrial cooperatives, business activities are undertaken. In artisans' cooperatives and weavers' cooperatives, they provide raw materials and other accessories needed by the members and the finished products are sold through the industrial cooperatives. The members get wage and dividend. In industrial cooperatives like, workshop cooperatives only facilities for manufacturing are provided. Purchasing of raw materials and selling the finished products would be the responsibility of the individual members.

**Industrial Cooperative Banks**

In many developing countries, cooperative banks have been organized in the field of agricultural sector. Sectors like industrial cooperatives are starving for funds due to the absence of a specialized industrial cooperative banking structure. To avoid such situation, in countries like India, separate industrial cooperative banks have been established exclusively to finance the industrial cooperatives. The industrial cooperatives raise long-term resources by way of issuing long-term bonds and debentures for a period exceeding 10 to 15 years. These banks provide long-tern credit to the primary industrial cooperative societies and they recover the loans through installments. Wherever industrial cooperative banks exist, in such places industrial cooperatives are prospering well.

**Weavers' Cooperatives and Artisans' Cooperatives**

Weavers' cooperatives are functioning in villages and they are keeping up the traditional weaving art. Like the weavers' cooperatives the artisans' cooperatives are also keeping up the tradition of ancient arts in countries. Of late, these cooperatives have started using improved technologies and they are able to capture sizeable export market also. But these cooperatives face several problems noted below:

***Shortage of raw materials***

Weavers' cooperatives are need of continuous supply of yarn, dyes, chemicals, etc. Many times, supply of yarn is disturbed, which affects the working of such cooperatives.

***Marketing***

Having outmoded technology, artisans' cooperatives area unable to find good market for their products. Even weavers' cooperatives, whose products are consumed locally, find the market very tough because competition is provided by the organized mill sector.

***Living conditions***

The living conditions of the weavers and artisans is very poor. It is the duty of the cooperatives to provide housing facilities, educational and health facilities to such members.

4. ***Technology upgradation***

These cooperatives care little to upgrade their technology to the changing conditions and the tastes of the consumers. If these cooperatives are not improving their technology, their products cannot be sold and they may have to become sick units.

**Problems of Industrial Cooperatives**

1. Availability of raw material at a cheaper rate is a problem for several cooperatives. Raw materials like coal, iron, etc., become scarce during certain times. During such occasions, the members have to pay high price for the raw materials or they have to stop production.
2. Updating of the technology of production is also a problem. Industrial cooperatives have to compete with private sector industries, which are updating their technology every frequent period. On the other hand, industrial cooperatives are not very particular to update their technology. This led to the suffering of quality in production and reduction in total production.
3. Industrial cooperatives need heavy finance of long-term nature. The needs of the industrial cooperatives are huge and the period must be long. Without having separate industrial cooperative structure, it is very difficult for the industrial cooperatives to manage long-term finance.
4. Marketing is a serious problem for cooperatives like handicraft cooperatives. The production undertaken by the industrial cooperatives is small in size and they are struggling to find permanent market. Further, they have to compete with the private sector. Without the help of government organizations, industrial cooperatives have to suffer a lot in the marketing field.
5. The members must be provided with latest technical training. When the technology and techniques of production are changing very often, the members must be given training in various techniques of production. Unfortunately, in many developing countries, the training is concentrated for agricultural cooperatives.
6. Government help is very much needed for industrial cooperatives in creating infrastructure facilities, raw

material supply and marketing. In developing countries governments have commitment to agricultural cooperatives and industrial cooperatives have been neglected.

7. Dormancy or sickness is high in industrial cooperatives. When members start industrial cooperatives, feasibility studies or business plans are not prepared and they start the cooperative with an initial enthusiasm. In due course, the interest is not kept and many industrial cooperatives face loss and become sick.
8. The success of industrial cooperatives, especially in the small-scale industries depends on the tie-up with the large-scale industries. In countries like Japan, the model of industrial cooperatives making a tie up with large-scale industries has been developed. The same thing is needed in developing countries also.

**Suggestions to Improve the Working of Industrial Cooperatives**

1. *Provision of raw materials:* One of the major problems faced by the industrial cooperatives is the continuous supply of quality raw materials. The governments can undertake this responsibility and provide concessions to the industrial cooperatives by way of organizing separate agency to provide raw materials to industrial cooperatives at a concessioanl price.
2. *Marketing facilities:* This is crucial problems for the industrial cooperatives. The marketing outlet is very dim for the industrial cooperatives. They have to compete with the organized sector. Again, it is the duty of the government to promote the industrial cooperatives by means of arranging better marketing facilities through its various departments.
3. *Revitalization:* In many developing countries, industrial cooperatives have become dormant and sick. Such cooperatives must be revitalized by means of providing additional financial facilities and marketing arrangements by the government.

4. *Lack of training:* When competition increases, that could be met by improved production. Improvement in production in industrial cooperatives can be done by means of giving relevant and latest training to the members. They must also be given training to operate new machines and instruments.
5. *Collaboration with large-scale industries:* The survival of industrial cooperatives can be improved by means of making tie up arrangements with medium and large industries. The entire products of the industrial cooperatives can be directly sold to them. This will avoid the crisis for the industrial cooperatives.
6. *Financial problem:* One of the major problems faced by the industrial cooperatives is the non-availability of long-term finance. The government must come forward to provide long-term credit to the industrial cooperatives or separate industrial cooperative banks can be organized by this sector.

**Scope for Organizing Industrial Cooperatives in Ethiopia**

1. Ethiopia has an ancient civilization and the handicraft industry is very old and scope is high for organizing handicraft cooperatives. Weaving is also very popular in rural Ethiopia. But the living condition of such weavers is very poor. Through cooperatives, the villagers can improve their living conditions and save the traditional occupations of weaving, handicraft, etc.
2. Industrial cooperatives can create employment opportunities for the educated and unemployed youth. At present, unemployment is spreading fast in the rural areas. By means of organizing industrial cooperatives in the rural areas, employment opportunities can be expanded to the rural youth.
3. Locally available agricultural raw materials provide enormous scope for the organization of industrial cooperatives. Agriculture-based raw materials and locally

available raw materials can be used for the manufacturing of handicrafts, art items, etc.

4. Handloom weaving is a popular industry in Ethiopia and industrial cooperatives can be organized in this sector. This cooperative can avoid the exploitation by the middleman and can provide good income to the people.
5. Sugar industry is a fast growing industry and sugar cooperatives can be organized on the model of India. Though sugar cooperative is coming under large-scale sector, such cooperatives can be organized to increase the living conditions of the farmers and villagers.
6. International NGOs are helping to create self-employment for rural population in Ethiopia. Such ventures can be organized through industrial cooperatives.
7. The federal government and regional governments are favorable to promote cooperatives in Ethiopia.

**Summary**

- Industrial cooperatives are organized by unemployed people, village artisans and technicians.
- Their main purpose is to provide employment opportunity, to provide raw material, and market the finished products.
- There are various types and classifications of industrial cooperatives and all types are having the main objective of providing employment opportunity to their members.
- Industrial cooperatives are in need of heavy finance and separate industrial cooperative banks are necessary to fulfill their long-term capital needs.
- Weavers' cooperatives and artisans' cooperatives are popular industrial cooperatives, which are rural-based and take care of the welfare of such rural population.
- The main problems faced by industrial cooperatives are, continuous supply of raw materials, updating the technology, shortage of capital, competition in the market, etc.

- If industrial cooperative are to prosper, they must organize separate industrial cooperatives for finance and regional and national federations to promote the marketing. Governments must also come forward to help such cooperatives.
- There is enormous scope for organizing industrial cooperatives in rural Ethiopia. Handloom weaving, artisans, etc can be developed through industrial cooperatives.

**Self-learning Activity**

Try to answer the following questions on your own:

1. What are the objectives of industrial cooperatives?
2. Explain in brief the working of weavers' and artisans' cooperatives.
3. What is the need to have industrial cooperative banks?
4. Discuss the scope to organize industrial cooperatives in Ethiopia.

# 16 Labour Cooperatives

A labour cooperative society is a form of organization for the employment of a group of workers who associate together for a joint purpose. The chief characteristics of labour cooperatives are the workers who choose their workmates, select their leader and divide the income in accordance with the contribution made by each worker. In labour cooperatives, the workers have the freedom to choose the type of work and arrange themselves for the execution of the work undertaken. Another virtue of a labour cooperative society is that the workers enjoy the freedom in arranging the details of the work without the employers' supervision to ensure that the work is carried on according to specification. The method of payment of its work is of the type of piece wage in so far as it is based on output. The Cooperative Planning Commission of India stated, "The most distinguishing feature of a labour cooperative society is that each worker assumes responsibility as the fair price of freedom and his only master is the work itself".

In foreign countries like France, Italy, and New Zeeland, labour cooperatives have been successful in different branches such as coal mining, agricultural works, queries, and public works. This form of organization fits in with the increasing division of labour in industry and with the tendency shown by the industrial undertakings to split up into a large number of specialized departments. In the West, three types of labour cooperatives have been formed.

1. Independent and autonomous societies.
2. Mixed societies under the direction of trade unions.
3. Societies under tripartite management of workers, trade unions, and consumers.

The first types of societies have been organized in France, Italy, and Switzerland. The second type is widespread in Norway and Sweden. The third types of labour cooperatives are found in England. Cooperatives for building materials exist in many European countries.

**Necessity of Labour Cooperatives**

The necessity and the factors for the organization of labour cooperatives in many countries are due to the following factors:

1. ***Construction activities:*** The increasing number of construction activities, particularly in the public sector led to the organization of labour cooperatives, which provide work to a large number of workers who are either unemployed or underemployed.
2. ***Adequate wage:*** Workers under the labour cooperatives get reasonable wages as they are not exploited by the private contractors. In addition to the wages, they get additional incentives like bonus, dividend, etc.
3. ***Margin of profit:*** The margin of profit kept by the private contractors are now transferred to the unemployed workers through labour cooperatives.
4. ***Nation building:*** Labour cooperatives help to construct the buildings and other projects, which form part of the national building.
5. ***Sense of responsibility:*** Workers assume sense of responsibility to execute the works in time and neatly. Because they are aware of that the name of their labour cooperative should not be spoiled out of improper work.
6. ***Homogeneity:*** The workers of labour cooperatives generally belong to the same trade, craft, and select their own leaders.

7. *Work contract:* They undertake the projects on contract basis and finish the work in accordance with the terms of contract.
8. *Their own master:* They are not governed by any employer. They are their own masters. The only master is the work itself.

**Definition and Meaning of Labour Cooperatives**

According to Van de Muyzenberg: "A workers' cooperative is an enterprise, a work community with a democratic structure and which is owned and managed by those who work within it. They themselves exercise control over their pay and working conditions and just as they decide how the produce and money, which they have themselves acquired shall be used, or as they divide a trading surplus (profit) according to norms, which have been agreed together and laid down in the articles of association (the bylaw)".

The following characteristics flow from the above definition:

1. The workers in a business also own that business.
2. They build up their own operating capital from savings and invest them in their cooperatives. The outside capital obtained has no influence on authority to take decisions or on internal power, both of which rest with the workers.
3. The means of production are controlled commonly, which are transferred from private to common ownership.
4. On technical, financial, and social issues, controlling is exercised on the basis on one-man-one-vote.
5. Management is democratic with consultation and decision-making in respect of general management by unanimity.

**Importance of Labour Cooperatives**

1. In any growing economy, there will be the growth of construction activities (private and public), which provide scope for the labour cooperatives.

2. Majority of the labour cooperatives engage semi-skilled and unskilled labourers. Thus, they provide better employment scope in the community.
3. When the growth of population is fast, unemployment will be a major problem, which can be solved by labour cooperatives.
4. Through labour cooperatives exploitation by private contractors will be averted.
5. Labour cooperatives can guarantee continuous employment to the workers and high level of wages to the workers.
6. The profit margin will be available to the members themselves, which will be distributed in the form of increased wages, facilities, bonus, etc.
7. Labour cooperatives will form part of nation building projects and construction industry, thereby contributing to the asset creation of the economy.
8. By executing the works through labour cooperatives, a sense of responsibility for the work is created by the members.

**Types of Labour Cooperatives**

Labour cooperatives are organized by different sections for different purposes. Cooperatives like, labour contract societies, transport workers' cooperatives, handicrafts workers' cooperatives, etc., are functioning successfully.

**Working of Labour Cooperatives**

The membership of labour cooperatives is exclusive for unemployed workers and no middlemen or contractors would be admitted to the society. The value of share capital is kept low in order to make the participation of all unemployed workers. The working capital needed for labour cooperatives is less compare to other types of cooperatives. Because labour cooperatives enter into labour contract of particular construction and they avoid the investment on materials.

Usually, materials will be provided by the agencies and only labour participation is undertaken by the labour cooperatives. The management of such cooperatives would go on getting orders ahead of time and see that no worker is unemployed and at no time the society is idle without work.

In many countries labour cooperatives prefer to enter into contract with government construction works and the construction work of cooperatives. In such cases labour cooperatives are given preferences in the form of priority for contract, concession from the payment of tender deposits, concession from taxes, etc.

**Problems of Labour Cooperatives**

1. One of the major problems faced by labour cooperatives is the continuity in getting contracts. During lean times and during the times of economic depression workers are kept unemployed. During the times of rainy seasons and natural calamities their work would be affected.
2. During the times of economic boom, they get work beyond their capacities and they have to forego many contracts to the private contractors. Next time, agencies may not extend the work to the cooperatives expressing their inabilities.
3. There is no assurance for continuity in the work of labour cooperatives. When a work is completed, unless they have other work readily arranged, they have to face unemployment.
4. In many labour cooperatives delay used to occur in preparing the construction contracts, payment of bills, etc. Such delays are taking place in government organizations and government owned corporations.
5. For labour cooperatives like handicrafts cooperatives, the major problem is marketing. They have to compete with the private sector who spend lot of money for promotional efforts.

6. Members of the labour cooperatives never bother about their future and they never indulge in savings. So, many cooperative do not have adequate financial strength. They make it a habit of borrowing from banks even for their working capital.
7. While entering into government contract, private contractors corrupt the government officials and overtake the labour cooperatives.
8. In many labour cooperatives, disputes arise with regard to the execution of works. Ultimately, this led to the earning of bad name for the labour cooperatives.
9. With regard to settlement of bills by the contractors (including the government) lot of delay use to take place, which affects the working of the labour cooperatives.

**Suggestions to Improve the Working of Labour Cooperatives**

1. Governments must make it a policy to provide at least one-third of the contract compulsorily to the labour cooperatives. On their part, the labour cooperatives must make it a point to complete the works in time and with perfection.
2. There are dull seasons and busy seasons in labour contract. During the times of busy seasons, the labour cooperatives must complete the projects within the prescribed time. During such occasions, they can hire outside labour temporarily and complete the project in time.
3. Government must give certain concessions by way of exempting the labour cooperatives from the payment of earnest money and security deposits.
4. Costly machines and equipments needed for construction must be provided by the agencies awarding contract to the labour cooperatives at a nominal rate of rent or rate contract basis.
5. Independent tribunals may be set up for deciding disputes that may arise with the execution of works and settlement

of bills because any problem to be taken to civil courts will be costly and may take long time. This will ultimately affect the continuity in the working of labour cooperatives.

6. While giving the contract, the government organizations must provide a portion of the contract money as advance money, through which the labour cooperatives can manage their affairs.

**Scope for Labour Cooperatives in Ethiopia**

Ethiopia is a country of agriculture. Industrialization is getting momentum. Even then, there is scope for organizing labour cooperative in various areas noted below:

1. In the field of agriculture, unlike other countries, there is no class, called agricultural labourers. But farmers can organize labour cooperatives and complete their agricultural operations in time.
2. Ethiopia has a growing population of unemployed farmers, who can be absorbed by labour cooperatives.
3. By forming labour cooperatives, government contracts could be executed by labour cooperatives. Government must make it a point to promote labour cooperatives and give a portion of its contract to such labour cooperatives.
4. Ethiopia has sizeable population of handicrafts workers, weavers and artisans who can be brought under the fold of labour cooperatives.
5. In Ethiopia, construction industry is getting importance in urban areas, and the urban workers can be brought under labour cooperatives to improve their livelihood.

**Summary**

- Labour cooperatives are very popular in Western countries and they are getting importance in developing countries.
- Boom in construction industry and government contracts led to the popularity of labour cooperatives.

- Labour cooperatives are needed to give employment opportunity to the unemployed semi-skilled labourers and to save them from the exploitation of private contractors.
- Labour cooperatives can be organized for construction labourers, transport workers, handicrafts workers, etc.
- The working capital of labour cooperatives is very less compared to other types of cooperatives.
- The management of labour cooperatives makes it a point to get the works continuously from government and other sectors.
- Labour cooperatives are given preference by governments in the form of priority for contract, concessions from payment of tender deposits, tax concession, etc.
- The major problem faced by labour cooperatives is the continuity of getting contracts. Several times, they get work beyond their capacities, during such times they can employ casual labourers.
- Ethiopia has enormous scope for organizing labour cooperatives in rural and urban areas.

**Self-learning Activity**

Try to answer the following questions on your own:

1. Discuss the special characteristics of labour cooperatives.
2. What is the scope for organizing labour cooperatives in Ethiopia?

# 17 New Wave Cooperatives/ New Generation Cooperatives

New wave cooperatives or new generation cooperatives are nothing but already existing cooperative or starting of new cooperatives, especially marketing cooperatives to increase business opportunities and value addition to the products. These cooperatives have been started in America and continued to gain popularity.

**Definition**

"These cooperatives raise the value of local farm commodities and natural resources, provide rural development and income opportunities and help stabilize the rural communities that foster them. Some of these new cooperatives reach out horizontally to produce new crops and products, benefiting communities through economic diversification. They create new jobs in communities and bringing producers a share of the proceeds from the processing of their products."

Cooperatives are sensitive to the business conditions of an area and the needs of its people. They bring together people, capital, business functions and services in effective, competitive economic units under local ownership and control. They are created and serve to fill an economic function and purpose.

From the 1950s through the 1970s, lack of economic performance by some cooperatives was often rationalized as a result of lack of cooperative education and understanding.

Education and understanding have their roles, but the real name of the game is economics. A cooperative's success or failure depends on how well it performs its economic purpose.

The rise of new wave cooperatives in the Upper Midwest of USA that began with sugar cooperatives in the early 1970s has become a virtual explosion. New cooperatives for processing and/or marketing grains, oilseeds, wild rice, potatoes and fruit came along during the mid to late 1970s. The 1980s brought further expansion and new cooperatives for such ventures as processing corn, marketing wine and providing financial services.

The 1990s have already brought new cooperatives to deal with aquaculture, new and expanded processing of corn into flour milling, frozen bread dough, pasta, potatoes, poultry and egg production, sugar beet processing, senior housing, sweetener marketing, vegetable processing and more.

The resurgence of cooperatives in the late 1980s and in the 1990s has been driven by economics, pure and simple. Opportunities are great, but successful new cooperative ventures do not spring up overnight. Large amounts of due diligence, time and hard work precede the startup of operations.

**Factors that Led to the Organization**

The following are the factors that led to the organization of new wave cooperatives in America:

1. The past failure of some of the marketing cooperatives.
2. Lack of business emphasis by the cooperatives.
3. Cooperatives unable to face the competition from private traders
4. Instead of winding up the cooperative, new thrust was given in the form of new wave cooperatives.

**Characteristics of Successful New Wave Cooperatives**

1. Value-added investment orientation to process commodities into higher-value products, moving producers further up the food chain.

2. Significant investment by members to provide the initial equity.
3. Defined or selected membership rather than open membership.
4. Long-term delivery rights and obligations of a specific commodity, with investment level tied to delivery rights.
5. Recognition that membership rights have value and can be traded.
6. Pooling of commodities and products with value-added payments to the members.
7. Expansion typically funded by new investment.
8. More frequent use of joint ventures and alliances.

**Success Factors for New Wave Cooperatives**

The following factors led to the success of new wave cooperatives organized in United States of America:

1. ***Local leadership:*** Cooperatives are successful if they're created "from the ground up". This requires local leadership with the vision, spirit, time and commitment to develop the idea, solicit the support and create the new organization.
2. ***Realistic goals and assumptions:*** Objectives of the new organization must be achievable.
3. ***Honest, open communications:*** All involved stakeholders must have a clear understanding of what is expected and how it is to be achieved.
4. ***Realistic market-entry strategies:*** Marketing the finished product is a major challenge for all cooperatives. For a new player entering an established market, the ability to market the end product successfully is critical to success.
5. ***Experienced consultants:*** New wave co-ops require experienced consultants for the diligence process– attorneys, accountants, lenders and knowledgeable industry experts who can develop reasonable and appropriate organizational structures and business and financial plans.

6. *Comprehensive business plan:* A business plan that addresses challenges and opportunities is critical in demonstrating potential for the project, determining required capital, raising equity capital and securing needed debt financing.
7. *Engineering and design:* Many new wave ventures are based on technology to process raw commodities into value-added products. Plant design and engineering are critical to successful plant operation and to production of quality products.
8. *Capable management:* Management must be capable of successfully implementing and managing a sound, comprehensive business plan.
9. *Sufficient member equity:* Owners will benefit most from success and must bear the risk. Equity capital from members must be sufficient to attract needed debt financing to support the entire business. Depending on the risk analysis, a 40 to 50 per cent member equity position is often specified for new cooperatives.
10. *Commitment to pooling:* New ventures are generally structured so that members are paid on a progressive basis as the crop is received, processed, and most important of all – marketed.

**Cooperatives Strategies by Adopted New Wave to Success**

1. *Providing new services:* As agriculture has adopted new technologies and become more specialized, producers seek additional services. Plant food and crop protection applications, crop monitoring, livestock production services and credit, are examples.
2. *Increasing market share:* In some cases, traditional cooperatives have increased market share through new product development, mergers and consolidations with other cooperatives and acquisitions of non-cooperative businesses.

3. *Vertical integration:* This strategy has often succeeded in livestock production where traditional cooperatives support production facilities in hog, poultry and cattle production. Additional dairy and grain marketing cooperatives have diversified and expanded through additional value-added processing and marketing ventures.
4. ***Adding value and diversification:*** The traditional federated and local cooperatives have created new organizations, including new cooperatives, joint ventures and strategic alliances. They also have added services to meet the needs of rural America, such as energy production and distribution, telecommunications and information services and local services such as convenience stores, restaurants and truck stops.
5. The new wave cooperatives embody the principles of the Rochdale weavers, established more than 160 years ago but modified to function successfully today. They are based on the successes of traditional cooperatives and the experience of the new wave cooperative ventures. They are serving well in rural America.

**Lessons from New Wave Cooperatives**

The phenomenon of 'coop fever', a term used to describe interest in developing new value added marketing cooperative serving northern states of USA, swept through Dakota and Minnesota states. The development of significant number of new cooperatives in the Upper Midwest with new member investment has created great interest around the world among those interested in agricultural and rural development. The lessons learnt from new wave cooperatives/new generation cooperatives are summarized below according to the activities.

1. I*dentifying an opportunity*
   *(a)* Reports developed identifying economic opportunities for value-added processing.

(b) Consortium of state leaders gather to promote further opportunities and set priority for development of agricultural value added businesses.

(c) Good facilitators to help focus on nature of the problem and opportunities.

2. *Building consensus on potential for cooperatives*

(a) Intensive support is provided through rural electric cooperatives to assist groups in assessing the potential for forming new cooperatives.

(b) Initial project planning includes the use of consulting resources.

(c) Projects are market-driven, starting with demand analysis

3. *Developing trust among potential members*

(a) Experienced cooperative advisors are available and utilized.

(b) Well-respected farmer-leaders to champion the projects.

(c) High degree of feasibility decided for proposed business.

(d) Experienced consulting firms are involved with matching funds for feasibility studies.

4. *Securing commitment from the members*

(a) Detailed quality business plan was developed.

(b) Well-planned and executed capital mobilization.

(c) Legally binding membership and marketing agreements.

(d) Leading farmers take the work of capital mobilization.

5. *Securing commitment from lenders and other stake holders*

(a) Strong member commitment require in capital and product delivery.

(b) Well-qualified manager hired early in development phase.

(c) Lenders who understood cooperatives.

(d) Well-qualified lawyers, accountants, and cooperative bank staff involved.

(e) Detailed quality business plan given to the bank.

6. *Starting-up cooperative enterprise*

(a) Effective execution of business plan.

(b) Anticipate start-up challenges (cash flow, management, etc).

(c) Board with a long-term vision.

(d) High level of capital financing.

(e) Business able to generate strong earnings.

## Summary

- New wave cooperatives are called as new generation cooperatives, which are very popular in USA.
- New wave cooperatives have given a new thrust to the working of the existing cooperatives by means of providing value addition to the operations.
- It is nothing but undertaking certain marketing and processing activities by investing needed funds.
- The main factors that led to the organization of new wave cooperatives are threat from the private sector, slow growth of the cooperatives, and a need to revive the operations of the cooperatives.
- The success factors for new wave cooperatives are leadership qualities, prominent role played by the consultants, new investment added to the existing financial resources and to face emerging threat from the private sector.
- The successful strategies followed by the traditional cooperatives to become new wave cooperatives are providing new service, increasing new market share, vertical integration, adding value and diversification, etc.

- The major lessons that could be learnt from new wave cooperatives are Identifying an opportunity, building consensus on potential for cooperatives, developing trust among potential members, securing commitment from the members, and securing commitment from lenders and other stakeholders.

**Self-learning Activity**

Try to answer the following questions on your own:

1. Define new wave cooperatives.
2. What are the characteristics of NGCs?
3. What are the success factors of new wave cooperatives?

# References


Braverman, A, et. al., (1994) "Promoting Rural Cooperatives in Developing Countries; The Case of Sub-Saharan Africa", World Bank Discussion Paper No. 121; Washington.

David, W. Cobia, *Cooperatives in Agriculture*, Prentice Hall, New Jersy.

Franz, C. Helm, *The Economics of Cooperative Enterprises*, The Cooperative College, Tanzxania & University of London Press, 1968.

ILO, *Cooperative Management and Administartion* (Second Revised edn.), Oxford & IBH Publishing Co. Pvt Ltd, New Delhi.

Institute of Agricultural Research (1988) "Producers Cooperative", Working Paper No. 4/88, Department of Agricultural Economics, Addis Ababa.

Kamat, G.S, *New Dimensions of Cooperative Management*, Himalaya Publishing House, New Delhi.

Kulkarni, K.R., *Theory and Practice of Cooperation in India, and Abroad*, Vol. Bombay: Cooperator's Book Depot, 1962.

Lele, U. (1989) "Markets, Marketing Boards and Coops in Africa", Discussion Paper No. 11, Washington DC, World Bank.

Miller, LF (1977) *Agricultural Credit and Finance in Africa*, New York, Rockefeller Foundation.

Malcolm Sargent (1982) *Agricultural Cooperation*, Gower Publishers London.

Maslennikov,V., *The Cooperative Movement in Asia and Africa*, Progress Publishers, Mascow, 1983.

Manzi, B., (1982) "Why Do Our Cooperative Fail", FAO/ FFHC, Ideas and Action, Rome, 146.

Mickel Brown (1995) *Rural Cooperatives in Africa, African's Choices*, Pengiun.

Munkner, H.H and A. Shah, *Creating a Favourable Climate and Conditions for Cooperative Development in Africa*, ILO, Geneva, 1993.

Nakkiran, S.A., T*reatise on Cooperative Managemen*t, Rainbow Publications, Coimbatore, India, 2000.

P.E. Lambert, *Studies in Social Philosophy of Cooperation*, Manchester: Cooperative Union Ltd., 1963.

Provisional Military Government of Socialist Ethiopia (1979), "Guidelines for Farmers Cooperative Development in Ethiopia", Addis Ababa.

Provisional Military Government of Socialist Ethiopia (1978) "Proclamation to Provide for the Establishment of Cooperative Societies in Ethiopia" Proclamation No. 138 of 1978, Addis Ababa.

Provisional Military Government of Socialist Ethiopia (1979), "Guidelines for Small Scale Industries and Artisans' Cooperatives of Ethiopia", Addis Ababa.

Tegene Teka, *Coops and National Development; The Ethiopian Experience*, paper presented for the FAO Workshop on "The Transformation of Agrarian Systems in Centrally Planned Economies in Africa", Arussia, Tanzania, published by the Institute of Development Research, Addis Ababa University, IDR Working Paper No: 18, Aug. 1984.

Tegene, T. "Producers Coops and Rural Development in Ethiopia", Paper Presented at the Economic Commission for Africa (ECA), Addis Ababa, Oct 7 - 11, 1985.

Wisconsin Center for Cooperatives, "Cooperatives: A Tool for Community Economic Development", Madison.

# Index

L



M